PRAISE FOR *JOURNEYING WITH YOUR ARCHETYPES*

Daniel Yalowitz is to be commended for tackling what is a difficult to describe, and a challenge to put into words: the process of individuation from a Jungian, and personal, perspective. The psychological ideas of Carl Jung, his "mentor from afar," has clearly inspired and provided Daniel Yalowitz' life and work and the gift of this book is to help us better understand these ideas in a down-to-earth manner.

—Aryeh Maidenbaum, Ph.D.
Director, NY Center for Jungian Studies

Through the time-honored image of a journey, Daniel Yalowitz invites readers to a homecoming. As a guide, he is seasoned. As a thinker, he is both practical and visionary. But it is as a wise friend that Daniel comes across most clearly, reflecting a lifetime of experience. His work with archetypes is timely and thoughtful, inviting readers to discover the possibilities of relating the mythic to the everyday.

—Michelle Lebaron, J.D.
Professor of Dispute Resolution, Peter A. Allard School of Law, University of British Columbia, Canada

This is a wise, accessible, and beautifully written overview of the archetypal basis of Jungian psychology. I especially appreciate the embrace of paradox, the unknown, and questions as openings to it all. As someone who has known Daniel Cantor Yalowitz for many years as a gifted professor of human development, education, and psychology, I did not know this dimension of his life, which is so close to my own. I was delighted to read *Journeying with Your Archetypes* and celebrate its contributions to our understanding of Psyche and the creative imagination.

—Shaun McNiff, Ph.D. Professor, Lesley University
Author, *Imagination in Action; Trust the Process: An Artists' Guide to Letting Go; Art Heals; Art as Medicine.*

Journeying with Your Archetypes

Journeying with Your Archetypes

The Search for Deeper Meaning in Daily Life

Daniel Cantor Yalowitz

ISBN 978-1-7327843-1-4
Printed in United States of America

Book design and layout
Booksmyth Press
Shelburne Falls, MA

Dedications

To Margie, who's been there and back for me so many countless times and has exhibited the patience of a saint and the concerns of a dearest loving friend and precious partner through this writing journey and all others for so long...

To Max, who has sat with me and stirred and purred me on, through thick and thin, never varying in his quietude and ability to settle both of us down throughout the writing process.

To Mom and Dad, who have brought me sixty-plus years of inspiration and love, tenderness, and high expectations and have never shied away from being loving parents and friends.

To all those out there who have served as archetypal companions for me along my Life Journey: I trust that they somehow know who and what they are.

Contents

THIRTEEN ⁓ Full Circle, Full Cycle

Acknowledgments

I never thought I would be able to write this book and call it my truth. But writing it has been an engaging and dynamic process. I think this has been the case for a few reasons: (1) I absolutely loved the content, and the freedom I was able to find to explore it; (2) I was sensitive and mindful about where, when, and how I went about the writing, reviewing, and rewriting processes; and (3) I had tremendous support from many people, and several beloved geographic places.

Odd or unusual as it may be, I want to credit my two homes, Greenfield in the northern Pioneer Valley of Western Massachusetts, and Wellfleet, on Cape Cod, for being the safe, quiet, nurturing spaces that enabled me to dig in deeply while excavating, then cultivating, this book from my mind, heart, and soul. They were silent and stalwart partners, from start to end.

When I first conceived the idea for drafting this book, the new millennium had barely turned over. I was in my final years of a 15-year stretch as a professor and administrator at Lesley University in Cambridge, Massachusetts. I had been teaching courses in this content area regularly there, my favorites being undergraduate and graduate level electives entitled *A Jungian Approach to Literature*, *A Jungian Approach to Fairy Tales*, *Archetypes and the Lives Within*, and such. Thus, my appreciation goes out to the many hundreds of students who took a risk to engage with me on this subject matter from an experiential and personal perspective. They were the many who initially helped to give rise and form to this book.

Going further back in time, to my first contact with Jung and archetypes and all other things Jungian involving depth psychology, my first mentor was the late and great Dr. Seymour Simches of the French Department at Tufts University. I took his courses, both in French and in English, he tutored and mentored me, I became his teaching assistant, and during his sabbatical he supported me in my teaching of my own variant of his work through Tufts' Experimental College.

I wouldn't have known to call Seymour my academic/intellectual mentor then, but I surely do now! Much of how I learned to teach, to advise, to care about students, I thankfully learned from him. The origins of my life-long learning as a student of all things Jung I gleaned from him. I have a huge and enduring gratitude to Dr. Seymour Simches of Tufts University for what and how he's taught me – what I now call deep process and deep content.

Seeing this book through to completion, I offer tremendous gratitude to all of my beta readers, who read and re-read, and responded to my many tough questions about bettering the writing. They are Phyllis Nahman, Rob Peck, Dr. Felicity Pool, Dr. Stan Bernstein, Dr. Allen Davis, Dr. Al DeCiccio, and, especially, my loving and loyal life partner, Margie Sobil.

Their reactions, responses, coaching, and appreciation kept me going further and deeper and faster than I could have ever imagined. They helped keep the process alive for me. Each of these people is a dear friend and colleague, and has truly supported the birthing and the journey of this book. I offer my deep and heartfelt appreciation to all of these loving individuals for the care they took to read, and point out errors, omissions, redundancies, and shortcomings. All wanted more stories, especially from within my life and world, and from the wider worlds of literature, history, and the arts.

Others with whom I've had both deep and informal talks about aspects of the book's content have helped me think it through with more precision and greater depth. This time, it was they who provided me with penetrating questions. I offer my thanks and appreciation to Chintan Modi, Dr. Gary Bernhard, Dr. Robert Cantor, David Yale, and my cousin of blessed memory, Jon Cantor.

I received sage advice and wisdom from a few local friends, published authors themselves. In particular, the encouragement and support I received from Marian Kelner and Sandra Boston helped to point me toward an excellent editor, Annginette Anderson, and a fabulous "everything and anything else" person who designed, formatted, and helped get the book into print, Maureen "Mo" Moore. No book is an island unto itself, and these new colleagues breathed additional life into the book and kept me moving forward.

I'd like to offer gratitude for my loyal, stoic, and silent partner during the hours and hours and hours of writing, who sat by me on the long dining room table, adding a gentle knowingness without ever actually saying anything: my forever furry friend, Mr. Max E. Katz, Jr., DBAAC.

Indeed, it takes a community to move a book forward into the world. In my case, there were an additional 15 people from seven different states, three different countries, and over seven different decades who helped to bring this project to fruition. Mere words can never do their love, support, and nurturing full justice; I send them my deep appreciation here and now.

Finally – I would not be here to write these acknowledgments, let alone the book itself, if it weren't for the ever-wise, loving, caring support and presence of my parents, Nat and Wendy Yalowitz. I got plenty lucky there! They brought me into the world, and that is the whole reason this book now exists.

One Final Note

In engaging with you in this journey with archetypes, I have one final note to share before you embark. In my renderings of both historical and current personalities in the arts, literature, film, music, education, and politics, I have deliberately and consciously refrained from engaging my particular views, perspectives, and opinions about their individual political stances. I have aimed toward impartiality in this regard, preferring to focus on their personality, their temperament, and the way(s) they may represent and symbolize specific Jungian terms, particularly shadow, persona, individuation, and archetypes. This, I hope, will allow my readers to formulate their own points of view without my having imposed my own political or other bias on them.

Preface

The Forward Journey of This Book

Like people – and all sentient beings – books have a life, too. This foreword is dedicated to bringing the journey of this book to life, in print. It's an important story for me to birth and share. Like the lives we hope to lead, this book's story has integrity, history, several challenges, a few failures, and, ultimately, as you see here, success (or at least a physical and tangible product and outcome). So here is what I believe the book itself would say if it could speak.

It actually began in college: in my first year, as an undergraduate student at Tufts University, I was accorded the privilege of enrolling in an upper-level course to fulfill my foreign language distribution requirement: a French course, taught in English! It was entitled, *An Introduction to French Literature from a Jungian Perspective.* What an easy out for me, I thought: I get to connect with upper-class juniors and seniors, I don't have to overcome my dislike of how language is taught in American schools, and I get to focus on literature from a psychological perspective! Despite being the oldest child of two social workers steeped in Freud, I wondered, Who was Jung? And how does one go about teaching, studying, and learning French literature through the lens of a Swiss psychologist?

Well, I got a better bargain than I could ever have imagined. I fell in love! This time, my newest rapture held a few things that were new to me:

- a new passion for reading literary masterpieces and really thinking about them, and writing papers not just to get them done and out of the way;
- rich, real classroom discussions where the students actually took the lead and the teacher actually listened and personalized his commentary;

- engaged, experiential learning where it wasn't only about talking and talking heads – we got involved in activities like psychodrama, guerilla theatre and Theatre of the Oppressed, meditation and Quaker-style meetings, and more;
- a professor who was an inspiration to me: Dr. Seymour Simches, my first-ever academic mentor, a small, slightly unkempt, wise elder Jewish *mensch* and faculty member, up there in years and with a huge heart, obvious genius, and fabulous creativity, who knew how to teach and was absolutely dedicated to doing so.

Seymour insisted that we all be on a first-name basis. We sat in a circle, all 16 of us, and there was no "head" or front of the room. He made this clear, first with words, and then, consistently, with actions and behaviors. We all loved it, and loved him for his honesty, integrity, and support of and love for the learning and teaching process. I worked harder in that course than for any I'd ever undertaken. As a social sciences person coming from a math and science high school, I didn't think it possible. But I learned passion, inspiration, and intellectual challenge from Seymour and Jung and French Lit like nothing else before.

Later, I was asked to serve as a teaching assistant in this course as a junior; my senior year, I taught the same class in the university's Experimental College, with a few new twists to the syllabus and the process, while Seymour was on a year-long sabbatical. I taught a college-level course on my own at the age of 21, while still an undergraduate! How very cool!

The fire that roared within me at that time turned to banked embers, but never ashes, in the years that followed. I continued to read Jung, joined a few local Jung groups, was a regular visitor and participant at the C.G. Jung Center of Greater Boston, and eventually became certified through Consulting Psychologists Press to facilitate the Myers-Briggs Type Indicator (MBTI©) as a trainer and consultant.

Finally, a dream come true: following my academic training and credentialing, I began what has been a four-decade career as an academic, developing my own courses at several New England colleges and universities. Seamlessly, or so it seemed, I was able to build, integrate, and teach courses with Jungian content, beyond what I had done ten years earlier with Seymour. *A Jungian Approach to Fairy Tales, A Jungian Approach to World Literature, Alternative Perspectives on Psychology,* and *Depth Psychology and Modern Life* found their way into the undergraduate curricula at these schools, and I started facilitating occasional weekend workshops on these and related topics as well.

The idea of writing this book was born during a half-year sabbatical, my first, in the spring of 2000. I had delayed taking the actual sabbatical for nearly three years while I directed a nascent program in Conflict Resolution and Creating Peaceable Schools at my institution. By the time I finally took time away, the institution had long since forgotten about my sabbatical proposal, so I really was a free agent, coming, going, and doing as I pleased for nearly eight months before returning. I journeyed to lots of fascinating places: singing with a chorus in Cuba, heading off to Costa Rica for sport and adventure, taking a family vacation in England, traveling for three weeks in Peru, including hiking the Old Inca Trail to Machu Picchu, and taking other more local trips. In the process I threw ideas together for a book – messy notes on envelopes, a precis or two in a journal, more reading and workshops – and called it all "professional development."

But, without any real internalized structure, this "book" remained a random series of idealized thoughts and fragmentary ideas. Good enough for the time being, or so I thought.

I tested my ideas with an uncle steeped in Jungian psychology, and he was both curious and a bit reticent with his responses to my partially-developed ideas. I didn't have many others whom I knew or trusted around this content, so I shelved the project, for years keeping it both "on hold" and buried as something I might someday accomplish. I went on about my life, and the dust collected on my notes and in my brain.

Over time, I began to doubt myself, and doubt my abilities to engage with the necessary discipline, though I did complete my doctorate. But a book? Open and available to the public? Perhaps most first-time authors experience this type of personal insecurity, but I felt particularly isolated, and, therefore, vulnerable. As I deepened my own academic career and ventured into higher-level administrative positions, the book came to feel out-of-bounds, on a life-long sabbaticalof its own. Over the years, I lost the thread.

But my interest in Jung and things Jungian – particularly archetypes and related concepts such as individuation, shadow and persona, and anima and animus, among others – never wandered. I'd see a workshop or course or lecture or personal/professional opportunity to engage in one or more of these topics, and I would find myself there, like wrestling with old friends "for the fun of it."

At some point, the interest compounded, much as a bank account accrues more cents (or sense?). On one particularly long trip I began to befriend – or "re-friend" – my interest in tying it all together. And I began to believe that there would be a sign, an omen, a life-transition that would allow this long-held but nascent dream to finally awaken: my own fairy tale...

Now, 16 years later – and, given another gift of "professional time away" following my departure from a senior administrative position at a graduate institute – I took a personal time out, spent a month at my cabin on Cape Cod, and *wrote*. I dug in: I now had the idea, the vision, the approach, the focus, and a specific theme, topic, and title. And, for three and half weeks, four to six hours a day, beginning at first light, I wrote. By journey's end on the Cape, nearly 100 pages of a first draft had appeared. I was amazed at how the book laid itself out before me. With almost complete freedom from life's "to-do's," I created feverishly. My self-sequestering succeeded beyond my wildest hopes!

Still, questions persisted. Who was my audience? Once identified, how would I engage them? At the 30,000 foot level, what was I aiming for? Was a book the best way to put myself "out there"? These questions hounded me as I struggled to develop an elevator speech, to concisely and precisely nail it all down, nice and neat. Once I returned home from my writing retreat, would my focus and energy carry me and my book forward? The cumulative effect of these queries was to erode my self-confidence – it wasn't nearly as clear a path as it seemed during my time on the Cape. I'd have to live it through to see it through – so I began to meditate once again, and came to see the book project as necessary and vital and hopeful.

In the twelve months between that September and now, I have applied myself to this task, to this love, on a near-daily basis. Stories from the past, *my* past, flowed as I wrote, and added fun and depth and dimension to this nascent book. They caused me to reflect, to go back in, to listen and learn from myself, and seek to further understand my life and my life's journey through a Jungian lens.

Friends, professional colleagues, and fellow aspiring and inspiring writers generously agreed to read drafts of chapters, parts of the manuscript, and eventually, drafts of the entire book. I received loving – and critical – feedback, generally constructive, sometimes over the top. I wrote, I re-wrote, and revised, added and refocused: the things everyone does with a book. To add to the thrill of journeying, I discovered that *I love writing*! And what you hold in your hands now is the product of my – and many other folks' – efforts to create a book that is an adventure and journey itself.

I hope you'll enjoy and benefit. Send me your thoughts, positive, negative, personal or not. I want to know your story, your narrative, your journey too! We're all in this life journey and adventure together!

PART ONE

ONE

~

The Journey

Who looks outside, dreams; who looks outside, awakes.
~ C.G. Jung

The Big Questions and the Journey

What are our lives all about? What does it mean to be a human being, and what is it to be human? These imperative existential questions have been asked since the inception of human thought and cognitive understanding. Of course, there is no single or "right" answer to any of these queries. Rather, we each offer a wide and wild range of responses based on our own life experiences and observations.

It is the uniqueness of our responses to these queries, and our own expressions of self-hood that give shape and form to the human race, with all of its extraordinariness. It is this delicate and dynamic interplay between the universal and the unique that brings form to our identities and our personal and collective journeys.

Yet there are a few universal experiences that we all undergo through the course of our development – a process the eminent Swiss psychologist, Carl Gustav Jung, termed *individuation*. We grow and, usually, we grow up – up in the sense of becoming taller, bigger, stronger, and older, but also in terms of being more experienced, and, ultimately, more adept at living self-sufficiently. A key aspect of our growth is that we go and grow through life as a journey – and a series of journeys.

In this first chapter, we will examine and explore the concept of "journeying," and the practical realities inherent in it. To comprehend what it means to journey is, in a very real sense, to grasp what it is to live, to be alive. Every sentient being who has ever touched base on our Planet Earth has been on a journey, or journeyed through life in one or more ways. Growing up means to journey. And journeys take many shapes and forms.

Most of us are familiar with journeys that involve a sense of adventure, of traveling out and about, of seeing things, meeting people, and engaging in physical activities. I label these forms of journeying as "external." For example, to date I have journeyed into and through 88 of the world's countries, exploring their terrain, their people, their cultures, history, geography, cuisine, politics, and so much more. However, our life-journeys do not end – or even begin – with external exploration!

The perhaps lesser-known, less discussed forms of journeys are those within ourselves: our dreams, the inner landscapes of our minds and emotions and feelings. I'll refer to these as aspects or elements that form our "internal" journeys. They are real, immediate, meaningful, sometime quite extreme, and always urgent for us; they touch and transform our hearts and minds, our lives and lifestyles.

We fear, love, enjoy, and are confused and frustrated by this inner mindscape. We try to control or manipulate it. It impels us forward, and it may also paralyze us. Throughout our lives, we move forward, temporarily enlightened, or we halt, momentarily frightened. Our inner journeys run the gamut from intellectual understanding to ultimate mystery. We each live within this rich inner way of being, doing, and seeing throughout our lives.

Through both our external and internal journeys, we get to know ourselves, develop our self-awareness, and build both our understanding of "other" and our relationships with other sentient and non-sentient beings in the world. In this book, particularly the first half, we will wind our way through an exploration of these journeys on a continuum from those that are universal to those that are truly unique.

Journeying in Time: Real and Imagined

To start, let's note that the first syllable in the word journey – "jour" – means "day" in the French language. In our human journey, time is a critical element, and a day is one form of measuring and calculating time. A day is something that we understand and accept as a common and universal concept. A day is both a human creation as a form of measurement and quantification of time, and a phenomenon of nature, basically measured from one sunrise to the next. As humans, we have universally agreed that concepts such as a day, an hour, a minute, and a second exist, and we have all manner of ways that measure them, backwards and forwards. Human history is indeed based on these and other measurements of time.

In English – perhaps in many other languages of the world as well – we have built a vocabulary of words and terms that have, in essence, commodified time. Let's dig in a bit here. To start, we often place an active verb in front of time, indicating a need or a desire to "do" something about it, or with it: *wasting, sharing, managing, killing, spending, missing, adding, subtracting, dividing, holding, marking, losing, gaining, giving, taking* – just a few among many. You can probably add others that you have heard or used yourself. Taken together, these point to the critical importance we place within our cultural and linguistic contexts on the meaning and purpose of time itself.

What each day looks like, and how we operate as humans within it, is, of course, a unique experience: no two people ever experience it in the same way. Even the human experience of a single day encompasses both universality and uniqueness in their arcs, from morning though noon, into evening, and completing the cycle with night.

Journeys occur both in time as well as in space. They can all be accounted for in both dimensions. The ancient Greeks had two words for time: *chronos* and *kairos*. While *chronos* refers to the chronological and sequential aspects of time, *kairos* speaks to the right or opportune moment – an indeterminate point in time when action is propitious.

Many of us live within a culture wherein chronos is understood and accepted. While some of us may struggle with aspects of time – being on time or in time, being prepared, ready, and anticipating the challenges of time – we have calendars that objectively seek to measure time in terms of seconds, minutes, hours, days, weeks, months, and years. Like it or not, our lives are regulated by all manner of watches, timepieces, clocks, and phones. Chronos is present, both in its micro aspect (in our personal lives) and in its macro aspect (the world's 24 time zones, and their relationship to one another).

Kairos is another story! Within time – any particular time – kairos gives us some sort of indication as to whether or when it is in that special moment that something most and best needs to occur. It is more than the objective "timing" of something happening: kairos tells us both when and how to be best prepared, organized, and ready to express or receive something in our world. As opposed to the objectivity of chronos, kairos is a subjective feature, its uniqueness becoming meaningful to each of us in a different way.

Most well-known and even universal examples of *kairos* are termed "rites of passage" and "rituals." A Jewish bris for all male newborns, a Catholic confirmation, our first day of school, birthdays, graduations, weddings, funerals, and so on: all call on us to prepare for a meaningful act that honors our culture, ethnicity, religion, or faith, or other aspects of our human identities. Which of these rituals and rites of passage have you experienced, or have you yet to experience?

The belief systems of various religions and faiths carefully incorporate the two different interpretations of the passage of time into these rituals. Practitioners within virtually all the world's major religions wear particular symbolic vestments during their services, whether by choice or per force. Rites of passage and life rituals must be carefully followed and carried out if they are to be correct and effective. There is an order, a *seder*, a structure, that must be observed, in some way or another.

All journeys – those within life, and life itself – draw on both chronos and kairos, and are often remembered for each aspect. Jung's autobiography, *Memories, Dreams, Reflections*, is a testimonial to this rich pairing. This effort, written just before his death, chronicled (another time-word, from the same Greek root word) his life, drawn from his own journals, life experiences, observations, and, of course, his reflections in and through time and space.

While it was written reflectively, Jung's chronicle was very much "out of order" in terms of the sequence and evolution of time and his life's forward movement. He was far more concerned with kairos than chronos: that is, he was far more invested in happenings and events, the special moments, markers, rituals, rites of passage in his life. It was achronistic – "out of time" in the normal sequence of life events. It took several of his intimates more time to reorganize his writing to bring a sense of order, clarity, sequence, and nuance (chronos) so that it could be read and understood with some fluency and fluidity, allowing readers to view his life as a coherent and cohesive narrative.

During our journey, many of us keep, use, or read journals – again, note the root – to chronicle our days on Earth. They may include experiences, observations, reckonings, and much more. Journals may or may not include the specific markings of time, but they do exist within a time-based context, whether or not time in the form of dates and years is mentioned.

Each day brings a generally understood and predictable cycle and arc: sunrise to sunset, among other things. As humans, we have created daily rituals that fit within this notion of a day: the eating of meals at certain times, perhaps religious activities or prayer at certain times, the workday, and so forth. These rituals may be factual, reflective, fantasy-based or dream-oriented, or poetic, or take many other forms and combinations. They serve generally to account for our time as human "beings" – and human "doings" as well.

There is a mutually beneficial – and paradoxical – relationship between a journey and time. On the one hand, each has the other integrally related within it. A journey can only exist within some sort of a time frame. And within a given time, there may be innumerable journeys. The length of time affects one's journey, and that very same journey impacts and influences the time it utilizes.

For example, an "outer journey" involving travel in a country new to one's personal experience takes place within a certain amount of time, and we may prepare for it accordingly. We must be careful to consider the emotional and physical preparations beforehand, the traveling experience itself, and the process of re-entry and resettling.

With an "inner journey" such as a dream or nightmare, or one enhanced by guided meditation or psychoactive drugs, time is involved as well: entry, experience, disembarking back to another form of reality. The experiences themselves, whether inner or outer, have an impact on our perception of time as well: for example, we may have heard it said that "time flies when you're having fun"; you may also have experienced how time seems to come to a slow-motion stop during a traumatic event.

Thus, time and the journey have a cause-and-effect relationship – but not only that! The two are, at the same time, distinct from one another. While time as a whole is at once endless and eternal and incalculable, most journeys are not – they are indeed bounded by time.

Most human journeys have an identifiable starting point, and often a midpoint. An individual life often has what is known as a "mid-life crisis," and there are countless other examples of journey mid-points. For some, a change in career or profession indicates this mid-life change; for others, a significant shift or ending of a primary relationship; still others have saved their pennies to purchase a new car or home or piece of art that helps them to redefine themselves. Some mid-life adults go back to school for another degree, or further their professional skills, training, and knowledge. Perhaps they've decided to embark on a big trip far away to see "what's really out there" and let go of their roots for a while.

None of these experiences are pre-packaged or pre-destined: they vary with our perception and understanding of our lives, our needs, our wants, and our dreams. Whether such mid-life crises are universal or culturally-bound is a curious and highly debatable point, one that must be determined based on one's cultural context or perspective.

Regardless of their cultural context, however, human lives come to a clearly demarcated end point. However we go about measuring or quantifying it, each human journey – from the oldest stories of humankind, including travelogues such as Homer's *Odyssey*, to modern-day fairy tales – has taken place in time, and has been marked by time itself in some meaningful manner. We will identify and amplify its differing elements in subsequent chapters.

Every generation has a way of marking its essential journey through life with epic or iconic moments. These may or may not have a cultural context and content attached to them. For example, for a US-born individual, depending on one's age and year of birth, this moment in time might have been the bombing of Hiroshima or Pearl Harbor, the assassination of one of the Kennedys, Martin Luther King, or Malcolm X, the first moon-landing, or 9/11. Of course, there are hundreds of other equally important historical milestones that potentially mark a person's journey within their cultural, religious, and ethnic histories.

We all know (or have learned) where we were "at that given moment" in time. It's as if our journeys halted for just that one moment, enough to allow us to freeze the frame and remember forever all the details and logistics of where we were when it happened. As a unique individual, what have the most special moments in time been in your life, and how has time or timing framed or influenced them?

Journeys and Motion

Beyond the journey in and through time, journeys carry another significant and universal component: movement, or motion. This movement may take one or many forms; it is the transition between two (or more) modes of action, interaction, thought, feeling, physical space, and intuition.

For instance, on a trip I made several years ago to Morocco, my physical modes of movement and transport included walking to the subway, to a bus, to a plane, walking to a second plane, more walking, a third plane, again walking, a mini-bus, and then, the next day, riding a camel. But these concrete changes in transport were only on one level, an external one; internally, for me, there was a long, and then a very intense sense of movement within me, spiritually and cognitively, to transition to another very different mode of being – an adjustment from Western to Middle Eastern habits of interaction and cultural context, from the known to the unknown, and the familiar to the unfamiliar. Time and space both appeared deeply altered at first, as they often do due to the unsettledness of travel.

Movement may also occur in non-physical, non-embodied ways. Some of us have traveled to the moon and back – in our dreams. Some of us have never been "out of state." Journeys may be still, without any physical movement at all. For example, our physical bodies barely move in our nightly REM dream state during sleep. However, within this stillness, our dreams move us in many ways, ways we cannot foresee or anticipate, and can certainly not control. These silent forms of movement are usually journeys of an internal and highly personal variety.

Movement is also minimal in other forms of "beyond the body" states, such as daydreams, trances, even journeying when our minds takes us through visions, films, music, and numerous other forms of media and non-participatory arts and performance. We'll reflect more on dreams and other forms of internal journeying in a later chapter. For now, it's enough to recognize that movement is a relative term that refers to the place (of knowing, of feeling, of traveling) where we start out, the places we head to, and possibly where we end up.

A note here about the inverse of assumed forward movement: being stuck, or simply not moving. In sailing, this holding pattern is referred to as being "in irons" – chained, in a sense, by not being able to find or catch the wind in one's sails, and then being stalled without movement. Similarly, in aviation, a helicopter or airplane cannot fly if it is not moving at all.

While it is assumed that any journey involves movement, sometimes the inability to move – or one's preference not to move – can hold tremendous suspense, mystery, and significance. Whether we are propelled by our own initiative, motivation, spirit, energy, or anything else – movement, especially movement forward, is not a guarantee.

In English, we have an entire lexicon to describe the idea of being stuck in time, in space, in our own heads, and in our feelings. Here are a few for your consideration – perhaps one or more may serve as a subtitle for one of your life-journeys: being stuck, temporary paralysis, unable to move, unable to move forward, feeling static or having a sense of stasis, being overwhelmed, feeling buried, burned out, or out of sorts. Sometimes the measure of our own mental and physical health is in our ability to remain resilient and hold our equanimity when experiencing one of these states.

Who of us has never been stuck and unable to move, paralyzed, as it were, by something in the present moment, a past memory, or a future-based fear? The pressure to move, and to be able to move forward, sometimes catches up with us. And, in the heat of the moment, while under pressure, we may regress to an earlier stage, state, or behavior. Might this have been you at one point or another in your life?

Allow me to offer one example of my many experiences of momentary regressions. I'll call this one my "fall from grace." Although I now see it as a ridiculous practice, my public elementary school annually named a student as valedictorian of the fifth grade graduating class. For better or worse, I was the young person so named in my year. From the top of that hill, I held – even became attached to – lofty expectations of myself as a brainiac and gifted learner, only to discover in a new middle school the following year that, in the eyes of my new teachers, I was nobody special, and I had to prove myself from scratch all over again: I was no longer the "top dog." Since that time, having sometimes unreasonable expectations and standards for myself has been a recurring theme in my life.

We must pause to consider what any of our journeys might have been had we not moved in a certain way – or to a certain point – at a certain time. The Hollywood film starring Gwyneth Paltrow, *Sliding Doors*, and Bill Murray's hit movie, *Groundhog Day*, are two excellent examples of the effect of a decision made in a moment, and the gift of opportunity to do things over and over again until we learn an important life lesson that we can integrate into our everyday lives.

Journeys and Our Emotional Selves

The experience of journeying carries a range of human affect along with it – sometimes as critical elements, sometimes as excess. These emotional responses and manifestations vary, from fight or flight responses to other less instinct-driven but nonetheless important emotions (love, hate, warmth, fear, desire, hope, and so on).

When I was 14, I proudly took on my first paid job as a check-out clerk in a busy supermarket. During my first week, I was held up at gunpoint and commanded to empty my money tray. Well: under the heavy heat of that moment, I got the tray opened in the register, and then passed out – I couldn't handle the pressure, went completely inside myself, and blacked out. I didn't take a "fight" stance – instead, I took flight, taking shelter in my deepest inner self without protest.

It is rare indeed to journey on any level without expressing or exposing some form of emotion. But with little movement, no speech, and virtually no outward emotional expression, my body took over and said what it needed to, perhaps saving my young life in the process.

Whether they are manifested externally or not, we all have a wide variety of internal (and often internalized) feelings. Journeying is a process that enables us to be human – to feel, to share, to express – or, put another way, to act, interact, and react.

It is also possible that a particular journey may cause or even force a person into a mode of silence or render some emotion inexpressible. Fear, for instance, may shut down external forms of articulated emotion because of the potential or perceived consequences. But, even here, we *are* emoting, albeit internally and silently – there are feelings within us, sometimes quite strong – even though they must, for a specific reason, be suppressed momentarily or well beyond a given moment.

As a species, if our individual or clan's survival depends on it, we have learned to "control" ourselves and even our emotional state, if warranted. The older part of our brains – our reptilian or limbic brain – has learned this over time. And we have been tamed through time and experience to utilize or control, as necessary and appropriate.

We all know and perceive trouble: we call it fear, and we respond and react more quickly than we can sometimes think about or analyze. In those moments, when our lives may hang in the balance, taking even a second or two or three to think and reflect may be too much, and we could forfeit our future for having taken the time to think at all. Jung referred to the psyche and our collective unconscious as a "cesspool of emotions". Have you or others you've known or loved ever been in this place? I like to think of emotions as being "energy in motion" or e (emotion) =e2 (energy) + motion.

Another aspect of journeying is our sensation of novelty – new places (in one's soul, in the world, in one's spirit), new forms (of hitherto unexpressed emotions, or visceral reactions/responses), and new observations of things previously not felt with any of our six senses. It may also involve putting things together into patterns for the first time, new understandings, or greater comprehension. Even while we may journey in the same ways to the same places, there are always new and sometimes incomprehensible circumstances attached to any given journey, no matter how commonplace it may have become to us.

For example, many of us have had repetitive dreams – "theme dreams" that involve many common elements – but, almost inevitably, something shows up differently (even subtleties like colors or lighting) and this may send us off in a new direction, even if it is one degree off course, and perhaps too slight to imagine.

For me, falling off the precipice of a cliff has been a recurring image – and, as Freud stated, I have never seen myself hit bottom, or experienced the moment of impact leading to my own death. But this repeated image has had varying backgrounds, of sunrise, sunset, an ocean or hard ground below, a hurricane behind me, or no wind at all.

In retrospect, having dreamed this memorable image well over three dozen times in my life, I have observed that it has most often occurred during a time of big change or transition in my life, when something in my world has felt out of control, or at least out of *my* control.

A yawn, a stretch, a cough, a breeze – anything added to what we perceive to be commonplace – can potentially catalyze us to set off in a new course of action, interaction, reaction – or inaction. We don't always know this in advance. We don't always get to have a "say" in how an experience or situation plays out for us in our waking or dreaming lives. So, novelty, like change, can be both a cause and an effect in the journeying process.

Even if we are unable to grasp its meaning, novelty is there, and it enables us to grow in some ways for which we may feel unprepared. In uncovering novelty, there is challenge – there is the unknown. How do we prepare? How do we respond? How – and will – we recover? Does experiencing novelty make us stronger, more resilient? How?

Films take advantage of these questions, sometimes manipulating them or their results in order to give us answers. Those wise enough to know better come to understand that there are no answers to these universal questions – only responses. As we've seen, these responses may be individual and unique; they may also come from within one's family, neighborhood, community, culture, religion or faith, or other aspects of our identities. How we react personally to a new experience is in the here and now, for one time only. Next time, there will be wrinkles in the newness, twists that we cannot see, sense, or predict.

Those films are exercises in ambiguity for many of us: we want answers, we want resolution, finiteness, a finish that completes whatever dilemmas and conflicts were brought forth in the core of the film itself. Yet we know that life, and movies, are not that neat, that clear, and that complete: we nearly always must come face-to-face with ambiguity, and the lack of clear definition that we want.

What Accompanies Us

There is at least one other consideration in the preparation for a journey: what do we need to bring along with us? This is distinct from the emotional and affective "preparation" we spoke of earlier. Instead, this preparation focuses on the physical realm of the material: tools, implements, supplies, the "world of things." What do we bring along? What do we omit? Where and what is the line between taking or leaving an object? And, how is this decided?

Think about the risk-takers adventuring up Mount Everest. There are at least two sides to each item on "the list": the extra weight of oxygen bottles, for example, versus the risk of going up into the thinnest air without such breathing insurance. The fool and the hero (archetypes we will spend time with shortly) travel simply and lightly afoot; the magician and the scientist do not. This is not judgment: it is need-based within and across particular domains, and archetypes.

Material objects may meet a need, supply comfort, or have other purposes: leisure, pleasure, tokens of exchange or barter, gifts. When preparing for a journey, all must be considered. However decisions are made, a journeyer starts off with some rationale for these choices. The decisions are unique. At another point, they may be based perhaps on common sense or common experience: a journeyer to the ocean might be wise to bring a hat; a mountain journeyer might conceivably bring strong shoes; both may need sunglasses and sunscreen.

On one of my earliest mega-trips – an eight-month honeymoon through eleven countries in South and East Asia – I recall packing, anticipating that I'd be in hot, sweaty, tropical weather as well as in high altitude deep snow. Out of inexperience and a desire to have multiple of everything, just in case, I overpacked so much that I spent the second night of the trip filling three boxes with "stuff" to send back home.

Finally, in the course of the journeying experience, one may well discard items along the way: on a hike on the Old Inca Trail in Peru to Machu Picchu, the well broken-in trail boots I'd brought caused major blisters after just a few hours. Finding them not only useless but painful, I threw them into a deep valley in anger and frustration, never to be seen again (at least by me!) and switched to Teva sandals and wool socks for the remainder of the journey. (The Teva Company *loved* that story!)

Surprises like these, as well as predictable additions and subtractions, emerge all along the time and space of a journey. Similarly, we add and jettison thoughts and feelings of a non-material kind along with the "stuff" of our travels. Generally, whatever we start out with is *not* what we end up with: there are nearly always serendipitous gains and perhaps challenging drop-offs and losses that we must encounter and respond to along the way.

Letting go is sometimes a matter of life or death. On that first trip to Asia, I arrived in Hong Kong in mid-summer knowing immediately that I had dramatically overpacked and would not cope well with the high heat if I didn't let go. Immediately lightening my load by nearly 30 pounds of stuff made that eight-month journey bearable and even enjoyable.

Inviting Paradox: Either/Or... or Both... or Neither

Let's pause briefly on this journey, to look back at the very essence of "the road." When we hit the road, so to speak, we are departing from something, somewhere, or someone to experience something leading toward something or somewhere else. Vague? Yes. At the start, all of what is known is the where, perhaps the how, and the when of the beginning. But clarity comes to us only in the act of the journey itself. The "experience" cannot be known in advance; it must be experienced.

In so doing, we must contend with Jung's notion of "the duality of opposites" – opposites coming together, rubbing off of or igniting one another, with results unknown until the experience actually occurs. Opposites are necessary to completing a whole, as with the ying/yang duality. Here are some of the dualities we have uncovered and discovered thus far:

- *The known and the unknown* (expectation and anticipation versus surprise and serendipity)

- *The concept of time*: Chronos and kairos, *"in time"* and *"beyond time"*

- *Physical and non-physical movement and motion* (the continuum from constant movement to total stillness, and everything in between)

- The *journey as a "container of emotions," holding more than one at the same time*

- *Modes of expression/articulation and/or expression being "internally contained"* (the relative fear or safety of being in "flight or fight" as a response to events and people)

- *Modes of interaction within one's self, or between self and others* (given that 85 percent of human communication is non-verbal)

- *Use of tools/materials – or not* (making conscientious decisions)

Intelligence and Problem-Solving along the Journey

Now, we turn to an aspect and concern that distinguishes our human journeys as authentic and individual: our uniquely right-brain areas of intelligence, creativity, innovation, and problem-solving. Without these, our journeys – sacred, profane, profound, and otherwise – would be more or less entirely left to luck, chance, fortune, happenstance, and fate.

Indeed, our right brain is unique among all planetary species. It provides us with the opportunity to "pre-flect," preview, review, reflect on, critique, and evaluate our journeys. As integral aspects of this process, the right brain helps us to choose a path that seems to offer the best possibility of success.

No journey, no adventure, no trip has ever gone precisely the way it was anticipated. Perhaps we'd prefer to know in advance everything that will transpire at every moment. However, to my knowledge, experience, and observation, life just isn't like that.

Perhaps that's why the human emotions such as worry, fear, anxiety, nervousness, and concern are universal. As we have seen, each of these may serve us as motivators, catalysts, and inspiration, as well as paralyzers and triggers for shut-down. In the end, it is in large measure our attitude that determines the nature and even the logistics of the journey itself. Thus, our emotional experience determines the process and outcome of each and every journey with which we engage throughout our lifetimes.

This being the case, then, we are more or less guaranteed that our right-brain wiring and skills will come into play on our journeys. Whether those journeys are internal or external, questions must and will be asked along the way. We've already witnessed several to this point. These queries bring forth our creativity, innovativeness, and out-of-the-box thinking. They also invite our trouble-shooting and problem-solving skills, and our ability to react and respond to any given moment and situation along our journey. All of our whole selves will affect the adventure itself, right on down to its core.

Drawing on Perhaps Our Greatest Human Gift

Journeys require our human intelligence. Our ability to draw on our smarts is critical at both predictable and unpredictable points. Think for a moment about some of the "classic journeys" in literature, film, and the visual arts – and the extent to which human intelligence has played a role of some consequence. Using film as an example, here are just a few to consider:

- *Oh, Brother, Where Art Thou?*
- *Forrest Gump*
- *The Wizard of Oz*
- *A Chorus Line*
- *Jesus Christ Superstar*
- *Peter Pan*
- *Titanic*

I think we could likely agree that these seven films are quite disparate and diverse if we consider plot, theme, characters, storyline, historical setting, and location. However, seen through the lens of journeying, they have much in common: a main character (protagonist), challenges that both beckon and threaten, and trouble brewing at several points.

What helps the main characters come through alive to each film's end is their ability to use logic, smarts, cunning, brainstorming, trouble-shooting, and, in a more clinical framing, their social, emotional, and multiple intelligences to negotiate the tough moments. (You'll read more on these final three in just a few moments.)

Now, think of your own journeys – a recent one, a long one, a deep one, a challenging one, a successful one – and whether it holds the same basic elements. When has using your intelligence made a difference for you in your life, and how? Or, conversely, when has that *not* been the case?

The good news about intelligence and creativity is that they hold tremendous new potential for all of us as embodied human beings. Long gone is the basic deference to IQ scores as the sole criterion and assessment of one's intelligence. Modern-day heroes in the movement to refine our understanding of intelligence – Howard Gardner, David Kolb, Daniel Goleman, and others – refer to multiple intelligences, and multiple learning and teaching styles as the modes through which we work, grow, and live.

When we are called on to solve or resolve a question or problem, we can turn with fluidity and fluency to one of eight forms of human intelligence, according to Howard Gardner's *Theory of Multiple Intelligences*: logical-mathematical, spatial, naturalist, verbal-linguistic, interpersonal, intrapersonal, musical, existential, and bodily-kinesthetic. Two psychologists, John Mayer of the University of New Hampshire and Peter Salovey of Yale University, built on Gardner's work to develop the concept of "emotional intelligence." Daniel Goleman popularized this in his 1996 book of the same name, and soon added two additional considerations to the "human intelligence map": social intelligence and ecological intelligence.

Let's journey into each of these three more recently "discovered" intelligences. They are not really discoveries in the classic sense: they've been with us in our human condition throughout both recorded and unrecorded history. It is the naming, the categorizing, characterizing, classifying, and defining them that has occurred only in the past 35 years.

Emotional intelligence, briefly summarized, has to do with how we understand ourselves – an "inner" or "self" knowing and awareness of what makes us tick, what ticks us off, and how we know the difference. Further, this type of intelligence enables us to distinguish between the inside feeling and outer expression of the continuum between these two. Our abilities to undo or repair the hurts we may cause others and ourselves are based on our clarity of knowing who we are and how we react and respond to incoming information and data from others and the world around us.

Social intelligence focuses on our ability to sort through and read the cues and clues of the people around us. Research tells us that approximately 85 percent of human communication is non-verbal. What does this mean? There are many forms of non-verbal communication; among those, two are sub-domains within the larger umbrella of communication: *proximics* and *semiotics.*

Proximics looks at how we communicate with others in terms of physical distance (how close or far apart we are from one another). Noticing this and responding to it appropriately, within one's cultural context, is one aspect of social intelligence. Semiotics is the study of how humans utilize signs, symbols, gestures, silent messaging, and other forms of unspoken communication. Again, our ability to "read" these expressions and respond in positive and appropriate ways – within our cultural context – enables us to interact successfully with others.

Finally, *ecological intelligence* pertains to our human understanding of natural forces, patterns in nature, and our interrelationship with them as humans. Clearly, there is a cause-and-effect relationship. The increasing body of research work detailing climate change is just one example of the impact that humans have on their environment, both locally and globally.

I had a good childhood friend who would run around to adults at our local beach warning parents to get their kids out of the lake quickly when he felt rain, lightning, and thunder coming on, well before others saw or felt it. In his adult years, he channeled this ability into a career as a major city weather forecaster; furthermore, he coined the term "the perfect storm" for the weather phenomenon that was later featured in a major motion picture of the same name. This is a clear example of Gardner's *"naturalistic (or ecological) intelligence"* at work.

Most of us are called to use our ecological intelligence to help us to problem-solve in our daily lives: how to dress and what to wear, what precautions we must take "out there," and whether or not to risk going out, driving, or leaving home without a hat or suntan lotion. Responding to these natural cues and clues requires intelligence and intelligent thinking, and the translation to daily reality.

We've come a long way in our understanding of intelligence and its human qualities since IQ tests were our one acknowledged form of measuring human ability. It is now commonly understood that, as human beings, we have the right, the opportunity, and the ability to move from one type of intelligence to another as needed. We may find ourselves stymied by our teachers, their teaching style and curricula, and the educational system or process itself, but that is a different story for a different book!

Each of us has a different "intelligence profile." Imagine a bar chart that shows a level of each form of intelligence for each person. This individual profile is strongly influenced by the relative degree of importance placed on each type of intelligence as determined by one's culture, cultural institutions (such as schooling), and family. We call this "nurture" in the age-old "nature versus nurture" dichotomy. The "nature" aspect has to do with the "hard-wiring" that we receive in terms of the RNA, DNA, and gene pools we receive from our parents and our ancestry. The integration of these two yields the particular mix of gifts and challenges that we work through during the course of our lifetimes.

There are multiple ways to consider the issues that emerge as we approach, enter, move through, and complete any journey. David Kolb's four learning styles (concrete experience, reflective observation, abstract conceptualization, and active experimentation) add further depth and dimension to our response to and interpretation of the many moments of challenge, choice, and change in the individual's journey, whether it be a journey into the soul or upon the soil.

In this chapter we've viewed the human journey through the lens of time, movement, our internal experience, and the tangible items we bring along with us. We have also examined the best piece of carry-on luggage we can bring along on our journeys: our own intelligences, in their various human forms. As we explore the fabric of the human journey in the next chapters, consider your own journeys (that were, that are, and that will be) in light of the dimensions we have discussed in this chapter.

Two

~

Embarkation

*Knowing your own darkness is the best method for
dealing with the darknesses of other people.*
~ C. G. Jung

Universality and the Process of Individuation

From our first chapter, you may have noticed that I am employing
the term "journey" in two forms: first, as a commonly utilized noun,
and also as a verb, "to journey," in all its tenses. As we deepen our
conceptual and practical understanding of what it means to journey,
it may be helpful to consider some actual journeys that we – as a species, and as individuals – have undertaken during the course of our
time as human beings. Using the "universal-to-unique" framework,
we'll start this chapter by taking a peek into a few different journeys,
in light of some of the elements described in the first chapter.

Part Two of this book will focus on the unique aspects and elements
that pertain to all forms of journeying. In Part Three, we will embark
on an exploration of Jung's concept of "archetypes," including what
they are, how we live with them, and how we can learn from them.
Finally, in Part Four, we'll circle back and reconsider the journeys we
first examined in this chapter to more deeply understand the roles
that archetypes play in our human life-journey and all the other
journeys embedded within it.

The one journey to which we are all entitled – and indeed guaranteed – is the human progression from birth to death. It's been said that the only guarantees in life are three: birth, death, and taxes. Some would contend that paying taxes is optional, but birth and death are not. In any case, other than the inescapable fact of the beginning and the ending, everything else in life takes on a meaning and a duration unique to each human being.

Our life-journey – the process Jung described as *individuation* – is one of moving from birth through infancy and into childhood, adolescence, young adulthood, adulthood, old age ("elderhood"), and death. As we grow and develop, we take on increasing independence and autonomy as we come to our personal values, behavioral standards, morals, lifestyles, and decisions around the choices, options, and opportunities we have before us. Many developmental psychological theorists have developed their own "stage theories" – different facets and phases of life that we all experience, and through which most of us grow and develop.

For example, Sigmund Freud developed a five-stage theory on psychosexual development. Erik Erikson spent his professional life evolving an eight-stage theory of socioemotional development. Jean Piaget established a four-stage developmental theory of intellectual or cognitive growth. Lawrence Kohlberg evolved a four-stage theory of moral development, which was later challenged and enhanced by one of his students, Carol Gilligan. Controversial as they may be, these developmental theories all make concerted efforts to look at "universals" – those aspects of our growth that seem to be common to all human beings.

The universality of many of these theories has come into question over the past generation of psychological and lifespan research. Regardless, we all journey through some individuation process during our lifetimes. In so doing, most of us emerge as independent and interdependent adult individuals capable of a relative degree of self-sufficiency and self-support – that is, autonomy.

This big journey of individuation poses significant yet surmountable questions and challenges. Sometimes we do not complete a particular challenge fully or easily: we may become overwhelmed, stressed, or stretched beyond our capacities, or lack enough support from others. Even so, life goes on, and we may merely survive, or possibly even thrive. Mythologist Joseph Campbell refers to our journey as the "hero's journey," and asks of each of us, "Where are *you* in your myth?" Indeed, whether we see it or like it – or not – we are the creators of our own personal myths, which combine to build a narrative or life story.

Many indigenous cultures around the world have developed well-prescribed rituals and rites of passage to delineate particular life phases. The Aboriginal Australian "walkabout" enables the young person to enter the journey of adulthood. Jewish bar and bat mitzvah students enter adulthood after successfully studying and reading from the Torah, as well as participating in other ritual actions. Ancient Celts, Romans, and Greeks had to manifest similar life events in order to prove themselves and make the transition into adulthood.

In most of these rites of passage, the individual is tasked with assuming novel responsibilities and activities, whether on their own or with others. The scenarios and challenges vary widely: physical feats, problem-solving, relationship-building, study and mastery, and even combat and competition with one's self or with others. The literature and research on this topic is vast indeed, with nearly every element and component of our full lifespan under consideration.

The Role of Consciousness and The Unconscious

The decision to embark on a journey is often a conscious and conscientious agreement within one's self (and perhaps with others) to take the first step. As described earlier, this proverbial first step need not be physical, but it does indicate a willingness of one's own volition to "step in." There *is* risk involved – whether it be a physical risk of known or unknown dangers, an emotional risk wherein a journeyer feels vulnerable, a spiritual challenge that might confront one's core beliefs, or a social or intellectual (educational) risk.

Hermann Hesse's unforgettable character, the protagonist in his novel *Siddhartha*, risks his fame, fortune, and security by leaving home and going on his own walkabout, seeking something beyond himself and the life he's known to that point. Several hundred years later, and several thousand miles away, I left the comfortable confines of my family, friends, and community in New York City to attend a large and highly competitive college in the Boston area, having to start all over again following a relatively successful academic career in high school.

In both situations, neither of us had a clue about what was next, and what skills and knowledge we'd have to draw on to problem-solve our way through the next chapter. This is the case for everyone who steps across their "threshold of comfort": to embark on the new and the unknown.

A well-known proverb states, "A journey of ten thousand miles begins with the first step." If one enters willingly, it is a journey; if it is not one's choice, it is – or may feel like – a "forced march" – a journey of a different type. Many years ago, I embarked on what I was told by the friends leading it was going to be a morning-long hike at Yosemite National Park. It lasted all day and well into the night – 19 miles and 12 hours. For me, it was a forced march; for them, an expressive, fun outlet. I was just not ready or prepared for it! When I ran a special education program many years ago, we had an easily-remembered mantra consisting only of two-letter words: *If it is to be, it is up to me.* The same is true of any journey.

We embark because on some level we feel ready for and desirous of growth and change, and the challenges they bring. Can you recall any journey you've made that didn't have a question or challenge attached to it? If so, would you call your endeavor a journey, or possibly something else?

The epic, historic, and daily journeys that have become part and parcel of the human condition and its legacy have all been rife with challenges, risks, and questions. These layer on top of the vast range of our ordinary measure of doubts, worries, anxieties, and battles of nerves. With all of them as background, we work to ready ourselves for an upcoming journey. We do so through various forms of physical, mental, spiritual, and cognitive preparations that are necessary to break out of our "cocoon of comfort" and head outward – or inward.

What makes this so challenging is that, as humans, we are also creatures of habit and routine. Whether consciously or not, we settle into our daily ways, and each of us develops a "threshold of comfort" that feels safe and secure, to the extent that this is possible for each of us.

Many of us learn to operate within this zone of comfort without questioning our ability to survive. Of course, those living in war zones or "hot" zones around the globe do not live with this security. In these situations, daily survival is indeed a journey, where the questions and doubts are raised directly on a daily basis. Whether one's journey feels life-enhancing or life-threatening, some of the aspects are the same. Some of us may not have the luxury of security, time, and funding to reflect and study, yet the character of human development and growth follows recognizable paths, regardless of the variables.

As with most aspects of our lives, there is both duality and paradox in undertaking a journey. Any imminent journey must necessarily involve a departure from the known, and a concurrent letting go of some part of our life that has been relatively predictable. Engaging in the farewell and the letting go is vital.

Any fears or anxieties during our forward movement into the journey may serve us in one of two ways: as energizers, catalysts, and stimulants or as inhibitors, obstacles, and retardants. Often there is a back-and-forth that occurs here.

For instance, I have been blessed and fortunate to have journeyed through dozens of countries to date. I travel because I feel a need to regularly get beyond my own "zones of comfort." Doing so has enabled me to experience a fuller life that has greater unpredictability, and therefore, more growth and challenge. I ask myself at least a page worth of questions before each undertaking, to be sure I am making the journey for appropriate reasons and am ready and prepared as much as possible for what may lie ahead. Never have my responses been 100 percent full-on "yes, I am fully ready."

I am well aware of the general ambiguity, even apprehension, I feel about these journeys. I often feel some degree of ambiguity about the precise reasons for my traveling, as I am not wholly sure where and when I will find challenges during a journey. By now, I accept the duality and paradox of embarking into the unknown with purpose and without a clear plan, but it still has the power to make me uncomfortable. The uncomfortable aspects also set the tone and potential to grow and stretch beyond one's former thresholds. With these challenges, mistakes are more likely to occur. In both cases, this is how genuine learning takes place within the larger context of our development as human beings.

The Role of Resiliency

How our journey plays out once we have entered it is ultimately based on two broad considerations: our attitude, and the extent and degree of our personal resiliency. Both are critical in moving forward our desire and readiness to undertake any journey of any proportion, as long as it is intentional.

The questions about attitude that we broach – ideally, both consciously and conscientiously – focus on whether we will be "successful," however we define the success of a journey. I always ask myself, "What could make undertaking this journey a success?" To find an answer, we must concern ourselves with the even more basic question of what the goal or goals of our journey are – if we even know. Of course, the way we respond – even whether we respond – to questions of logistics and details is based on our attitude.

Regarding our unique sense of personal resilience, two factors are in play: day-to-day or *operative* and *functional resilience* and longer-term, broader-issue or *personality resilience*. Both contribute to our ways of being and our ways of doing. In fact, they play off one another, much in the same manner as yang is embedded within yin, and vice versa. These two elements are separate and distinct, and yet always operate within the broader context of one another.

Resilience is our ability to bounce back from life's hits and hurts, from our defeats, challenges, and struggles. Humans are remarkably resilient; we can observe and experience any number of examples in our daily lives. Resilience is not just around us, but within us as well! It is not all that different than resolve or determination – the logical ways we respond to and manage the minor and major stressors, obstacles, and inconveniences that are part of the human experience. These challenges are often catalyzed or enhanced through the specific experience of a journey.

Your story is an important one to consider in this light. Not one of us would be who and where we are today if not for the quality of resilience. When I think about the number of times I have become unwell, even quite ill, during my international travels, and the lack of quality medical care available in many places, I think of luck, good fortune, and angels on my right shoulder. And yet, were it not for my own resiliency, who's to say how and to what extent I would have been able to bounce back to my *everyday* self? Consider a time when you've attributed your successful outcome of a journey to luck, good fortune, and the kindness of others and how this may have influenced your own sense of resilience. How does the opportunity of one stack up against the capacity of the other?

With regard to "operative" and "functional" resilience, on any given day, at any given moment, we may feel and present ourselves to be highly resilient – or the total opposite. This might be best described as the "short form" of human resilience, as these fluctuations have as much to do with our momentary energy reserves as our motivation to "do" something rather than simply "be" with ourselves – or anyone else.

This type of operative or functional resilience has everything to do with the here-and-now, with our momentary capacity to move forward. The time elapsed since we last ate, our last conversation with a friend or family member, the weather and time of day, and how much sleep we got the night before – all have everything to do with the degree of this resilience.

The "long form" of human resilience has more to do with our personality, our temperament, our values, and the other brush strokes of our life that are broader and fuller than our energy in the moment. Personality resilience is subject to far less fluctuation than its complementary opposite. Our human personalities are built, measured, and evolved over the long haul of our lives. At any particular point in time, our personality resilience is the sum total of the reserves that we bring along to engage us in the journeying experience.

It is our very resilience that allows us to take risk: going on a journey, as we have seen, often involves not knowing its process, its perils, or its outcome. Without some degree of inner or psychic confidence, most of us would probably just as soon stay home. Jung called one of his most perilous journeys his *"Night-Sea"* journey, a voyage fraught with peril, fear, the unknown, and lack of clarity, perception, and understanding. Another way of perceiving this event is as a *"might-see"* journey – as in, we "might see," or we might not.

We can undertake our journeys either consciously or unconsciously. At the same time, we cannot manipulate them – that is, we cannot mitigate the risk by anticipating all possible outcomes. The risk is precisely in bringing ourselves to the precipice, without knowing the risks – if any – that may be involved. Sure, we can involve ourselves intellectually and delve into the potential positives and negatives involved in venturing out and forward (backward too – sometimes our journeys bring us back in time, as well, to revisit treasured or haunted memories, people, and places!). But at the same time, we are neither omniscient nor omnipotent.

As such, we cannot know nor contain everything that may come to pass in our undertaking. Nor can we skip through steps, phases, stages, or chapters of the journey. It plays out as it must, as it is meant to – and therein lies the rub and the risk.

To Risk... or Not?

For many – perhaps for you – there is excitement, stimulation, challenge, and "alive-ness" in stepping forward into a risky journey. To risk, one might say, "*Bring it on*," and, in so doing, might "let it all go." Others may experience a journey more indirectly and vicariously: some might question or even attack us for taking it on, others issue a "thumbs up" along with a resounding "*Go for it!*"

You may have heard and possibly been part of conversations about the all-too-human issues of personal power and control. Who has them? And – when? Who maintains them and who passes them on? Questions abound, and, usually, the responses are clear – and, often, beyond us. Most of us see power and control in our lives as being held by others who are either directly or indirectly connected to our personal life experience.

Thus, when we act (and journeying is nothing if not a set of actions, whether in one's mind or with one's feet), we take a risk, whether with a lower-case "r" or a capital one. If a journey transpires from a place of consciousness, even conscientiousness, then it may be said that the point of embarkation is that moment when we acknowledge that we are ready, that we are no longer inactive from a sense of paralysis, but, rather, are now thrusting ourselves into active duty, and due diligence.

Let's be sure not to cast an overly negative attitude over risk, however. As humans, risk often seems hard-wired right into the core of our DNA, since we are by nature curious beings. We want to know more; we are hungry for experience; we seek exposure to the novelty that the world offers us.

As newborns, infants, and toddlers, each day is fraught with risk – except we lack the language at that sensitive age to call it that. What do infants and newborns cry about? Their tears come from hunger, for sure (both physical and psychoemotional) – but also exhaustion, discomfort, and fear. Fear can be both a motivator and a paralyzer for human activity. It is the same for risk.

Newborns and infants lack the intellectual capacity to do what adults often do, which is to perform a conscious "risk-benefit analysis" before taking a risk. Many of us feel compelled to chance things, and most often we do so because we perceive that the potential benefits and gains will outweigh the potential losses. We'll revisit this in a different context later on in this book. Do we leave a job before we have agreed to our next position? Risky – and possibly liberating – and a highly individual decision.

Because it is in our very nature to grow, to strive, to build, enhance, and refine aspects of ourselves and our lives, it is also in our nature to assume risk on some level in order to reap the possible benefits. Were it not for this upside, risk would indeed be more of a dark, even clandestine concept or pragmatic reality than it is.

Years ago, I arrived solo at the south rim of the Grand Canyon, exactly 100 days after double arthroscopic surgery on my right knee. I had rehabbed to the point where three doctors agreed to allow me to try the one-day-down, next-day-back-up hike to Phantom Ranch on the bottom of The Canyon, by the Colorado River. But none of us really knew how my knee and my body would respond. The night before, I came to the rim and saw Phantom Ranch from far above, at least a million or more miles from where I stood. A large, warm tear rolled slowly down my chilled cheek. I was freaked out about my chances – was the risk beyond me?

I was initially surprised to feel that tear, and I sat and talked with love and care to myself, saying it *was* worth the risk: I really wanted this experience, no matter what. At that moment, I was pleased to also note that I had grown to the point where I could consciously recognize my own fear, acknowledge it, and move into risk-taking anyway. The tears may well have represented an internal conflict between my functional resilience and personality resilience. And so, my desire, motivation, and internal fortitude and resilience came to the fore, and I lived the risk and had an incredible journey, both emotionally and physically!

As we've seen, risk is really about two basic things: (1) our readiness – or perception of readiness – to undertake some degree of novelty; and (2) a statement to ourselves and the outer world that we are about to move into action with something that has no guaranteed outcome or conclusion. As we have already considered the former, let's now regard the latter.

How - and Can - We Prepare?

When we prepare to undertake a journey, we have come to grips with the notion that we are about to move from inaction to action. This is a form of "arrival" – we have actually already come from somewhere to a new, other place. In arriving at this new place – the precipice of action – we often draw on our emotion, especially if we see "e-motion" as being energy ("e") in motion. Our personal resilience may come into focus and play a significant role for us as we enter our journey at this beginning point.

Psychic or soul journeys – such as Jung's "Night-Sea Journey" – often take place when we are in a raw or ragged emotional state. At such a time, we are not in full control of these emotions. Our soul or psyche rumbles forward without its familiar "editor" to calm it or slow it down.

Similarly, physical journeys involving our bodies happen following a time of preparation, no matter how brief. In either event, the *prima materia* – the prime matter within us – has gone through a period of germination, of catharsis, in order to allow for embarkation. Within the bigger dream and yearning for the journey to come, we must plan and prepare, planting smaller seeds among the larger growth of a dream-to-be and the journey to be undertaken.

This preparation for embarkation may come in many forms and formats, all on a continuum ranging from neatly contained to chaotic. Visually, it is more complex than one *or* the other. This was not lost on Jung: one of his fondest expressions was to remark, "It is surely not a question of one or the other, but, rather, whether we can accept the notion of one *and* the other." As such, journey preparation and embarkation might look like the symbol of yin and yang – each having a small portion, a seed, of the other contained within itself.

As we make our preparation for embarkation, we work on two major levels, and, within them, several sub-levels as well, in a process that integrates both the physical and psychic aspects of preparation and actual embarkation. It's important to note here that preparation – the how and the what – has an impact on embarkation and explores the "why" as we engage more deeply in the process.

The most physically evident of the two major levels of preparation is the *conscious* level, where we are organizing the multiple logistics and details of the journey. This comes to some of us more naturally than to others. We all fall somewhere along a continuum in organizational activity and ability. One end of this continuum or scale might be considered neurotic – perhaps an overly obsessive and even burdensome approach to embarking on a journey. Think about the way you pack for a short or long journey. What is your process (if indeed there is a "process"!) for doing so?

On the other side of this continuum – the other extreme – might sit the notion of chaos: an inability to organize logistics in a timely manner, which might hinder the preparation and embarkation processes.

To be clear, none of us always sits on one end or the other of this continuum. We humans, with our varying motivations and resiliency levels, are far more complex than this. And, to a certain extent, where we sit on the neurotic-to-chaotic continuum also depends on the type of journey to be experienced.

Some journeys are more in keeping with our own previous experiences, successes, and even neural pathways; others are a stretch. An example might be finding a new way to walk to school: we've been there many times, perhaps always via a well-known route. But, in the event of a change, the walk becomes a new and novel adventure, a journey: it's an altogether different experience. If there is even a little resistance or hesitancy, we may find that our normal preparations (in keeping with our other life experiences) are negatively affected; on the other hand, a particularly exciting or stimulating journey may overrule the chaos that we would more typically experience with our preparations for embarkation.

On a deeper level, our readiness to embark on a journey is also a matter of our *unconscious*. By definition, we are unaware of whatever is unconscious. Thus, beneath the conscious, demonstrable preparation for a journey, there lies a vast core area of psychic or soulful emergence that we have little conscious control over. Have you ever noticed that your dreams are bigger and clearer – and perhaps more eruptive and evocative – on the night before a journey or major life experience than at other times? This speaks to the unconscious activity that helps or hinders our emotional readiness for departure.

Dreams are only one psychic, unconscious manifestation of this feature at work. Others may involve forgetfulness (or its opposite, hypervigilence), overreaction (or nonreaction) to something thought previously benign, or what might be called *restimulation*, when we are triggered by things or people from our past that might otherwise ordinarily pass right on by.

For example, I may be restimulated when I see someone crossing the street who, to me, is the spitting image of my father (or mother, or one of my grandparents): they remind me of the storehouse of my memories, actions with, and reactions to that person and our relationship. This, then, "triggers" an emotion, positive or negative, that I project onto the other person. Of course, they know nothing about what's going on for me, and have no idea how to respond if my words or behavior are inappropriate to the moment.

We are restimulated by more people and things and images in our sensing fields (touch, sight, sound, taste, smell) than we are fully conscious about. Most often, we are unaware of or unconscious about our restimulations and our responses or reactions. Frequently, when we are in the grip of a moment of restimulation, it takes a dear friend or a momentary action of consciousness to "catch us up to the moment"; consequently, we may seem genuinely surprised that we did or said something from that triggered place. Have you ever said something to the effect of, "I have no idea why I did/said that" or "I don't know how that came over me." These are statements of restimulation – and they are thoroughly and unconditionally human.

The "Awareness Balance": Conscious and Unconscious

If consciousness is the top 10 percent of the iceberg of our human awareness, then the remaining 90 percent lies beneath, and is potentially eruptive at moments we might consider least opportune or most surprising. Jung labeled that which lies underneath the surface of our consciousness as the *"collective unconscious"* – more on this soon. Developing greater awareness of our collective unconscious will help us to better understand the second element in our psychic and/or our physical journey: our personal preparation and embarkation.

We are moved to the precipice of embarkation by forces both known and unknown to us. We might consider the question, "Why am I moved – or moving – to undertake this journey now in my life?" Our reflections, responses, or answers indicate that we may or may not have thoughtful and discerning insight. We may "know," or we may not. This may be because a great deal is germinating below the surface and has not yet been forced into our conscious awareness. In time, it might be. It may also be deeply intuitive, in a way that we might not ever be able to discern or explain, and yet, we sense it and know it.

But journeys do not wait for the perfect moment. We embark because it is "time" to do so: someone else's external schedule, our own internal time frame, happenstance, opportunity, or possible loss or abandonment if we do not. Even conscientious planning and preparation might leave out an aspect of readiness that we weren't concerned about: the potential effect or impact on another person in our circle, or a consequence that we had never considered.

We cannot possibly know all that is about to transpire for us and others connected to us when in the preparation and embarkation stage. But we plan, we prepare, and we journey because something within tells us it is time to do so – recall the earlier expression, "If it is to be, it is up to me." The well-popularized Latin phrase, "*Carpe diem*" (seize the day, or live for the moment) speaks to this as well. When Sir Edmund Hillary was asked, "Why climb Everest?", his famous and cryptic response was, "Because it is there." This is not unusual. It says a lot, and at the same time, it says not much. We live, we are moved to embark, we prepare, and we depart within this bifurcated and dualistic framework.

~

THREE

The Journey Cycle, Part I: The Request

A Few General Opening Thoughts

Preparation and embarkation are ongoing. They peak in importance as the first stages and phases of our journeying emerge. But they don't complete themselves immediately after we depart for a journey. As with any other experience in life, we may come back to the beginning, for any number of reasons. Challenges, obstacles, changes in perspective and attitude, and even benefits and gains made during the journey – all can cause us to revisit our starting place. We may want – or choose or need – to reset and recalibrate or reconnect to ourselves or to our sense of place and time.

The importance of context to any journey cannot be overstated. Context always has a beginning, a starting place. And so when, whether by choice or need, we find ourselves asking the same questions all over again, this first aspect of our human journey is recycled.

How many of us, as adults, have come back to reading children's books in later years, and discovered and discerned yet more wisdom and richness from a second, later reading? Some of my favorite books come from earlier times: *The Little Prince, The Phantom Toll-*

booth, The Wizard of Oz books, Alice in Wonderland, The Wind and The Willows, Lord of the Rings, and others.

For an earlier generation of Americans, it may well have been the *Nancy Drew* book series. I would imagine that, for this most recent generation, it was the *Harry Potter* series. Each generation has its own journey-books that offer at least two things: they transport their readers into a new world (the future and its potential) while also bringing them back in time to revisit old, safe, and comfortable or known places, times, and characters.

The Content and Context of the Request

Whether we cycle through or return to the preparation and embarkation stages, there is so much to experience as we journey onward. Our readiness takes us into the largest element of a journey: the "quest." We'll spend time in this chapter considering the quest, just as we do in our journeys themselves.

First, however, let us explore a subtheme to the quest, which conveniently and appropriately I call the "request." How odd that the prefix "re" – which generally means "again" – comes first! But elaborating on this "request" must be honored before we can discuss "questing."

To request usually means to ask for something from someone else. It entails anticipation, possibly fear, and the unknown. In requesting something of someone, we become at least temporarily subservient to them: they have something we want or need. This disparity engenders the question we must ask of them – the "request." In journeying, this question takes the form of hoping for an item, an emotion, a response, information, or a service that will further us on our journey's way.

Perhaps this request is for "safe passage." I'd like to share two brief moments from my past that I share with friends and strangers with a sense of "gallows humor": I once heard two pilot friends say this about flying in airplanes: (1) The only thing that makes a plane fly is the collective belief of its passengers that it will do so, successfully;

and (2) One's PFD ("personal flotation device") is the person sitting next to them (this from a bush pilot in the deep Alaskan wilderness, as I was planning to board his bush plane!).

In response to both of these, I found myself making the same request (or prayer!): "Let us make this journey safely, and land on the other side without incident." Many fairy tales include this same request: the child asks of the adult if they may have some token (breadcrumbs, for example, in *Hansel and Gretel*) to lead the way and ensure "safe passage" on the way back home.

Sometimes, the request made of others is simply an asking for something, and it may be offered, or not. On other occasions, the response to the "ask" may have conditions attached: "If I give you this ('a'), then I want that ('b') in exchange." Or it could be a barter of one item or service for another service or item. It may be a "question-and-response" situation, a negotiation, or even a mediation ("I will offer you this if you can donate/lend, or give me that…").

One example of this from another fairy tale takes place when the little man in the Rumpelstiltskin story asks the mistress miller why she is crying, and she responds by stating that she must spin straw into gold or die. Desperate, our gold-spinning girl offers him her necklace if he'll spin the straw into gold for her. Good, but not good enough: as the greedy king now desires more gold, she must barter her precious ring and then finally the promise of her firstborn if she survives and becomes the King's Queen. Were these giveaways too high a price for her to become the wife of the King, or not?

We make requests in a timely fashion prior to a journey in the hope that they will receive a thoughtful, respectful, and timely response – but it's not always the case. There are so many ways that a request may be made, received, and, finally, given a response.

The request is sometimes made manifest through our behaviors, utterances, or offerings. We bargain for whatever it is we believe will best position us for the journey itself. Sometimes it is the need for an item left behind pre-departure, or forgotten or needing to be found, obtained, or attained along the way. Sometimes it is a spoken or silent prayer for something we cannot attain or obtain itself (ever wish for good weather on a very special day?). The request is about wish-fulfillment made real on some level, in order to transition and position us for the full thrust of our journey – the "quest."

The Quest: Stepping In, Reaching Out

Often making the request is not simple or immediately clear. We may find ourselves wrestling with the vulnerability involved in the suggestion that we "need" something – whatever it may be – that is out of our hands and beyond our control. This "letting go" of whatever powers we perceive we have is itself a highly charged moment. It involves commitment and dedication: The journey of ten thousand miles begins with the first step. From the moment of the ask through whatever response or answer is returned, we are vulnerable. To make a sincere request can be scary, elating, nerve-wracking, joyous – or any combination of these.

The very "stepping in" engages us, in that we have made an active de-cision – in the form of either physical action or psychic and soul-fu-eled thought – to take this journey. We are on the precipice, and, while powered by the energy to move forward, we may yet have lingering doubts in the form of questions that identify our human vulnerability: "Can I do (succeed in) this?" and "Am I (whatever) enough to take this on, here and now?"

In these opening moments of the journey, we are essentially request-ing something of ourselves – to take (or bring) ourselves to a higher level. The young novice Maria in *The Sound of Music* provides a clear example of this. She prays (while singing at the top of her voice) for confidence and "the courage I lack" before arriving at the Von Trapp estate to start her job as governess. Thus, self-confidence may mingle with elements of self-doubt, in some precarious balance. All this is understandable, and completely human and natural.

Psychologically speaking, the launching of our journey holds within it the very question of whether we are capable of the launch itself

– just as the yin contains the yang, and vice versa. Fear (as well as excitement) may creep in, and may either catalyze or paralyze us. At this point, much depends on the sense of viability and resilience that we explored earlier. We must remember: as creatures of habit, it is fully within our human conditioning to question and query.

We all have our habits and our routines, and, to a certain extent, we grow comfortable inhabiting and making them manifest every day. The request can defeat us – it can be that powerful. Rejections are always potentially helpful. Most of the time, they can serve us as learning experiences. From them, we can develop greater resilience, possibly reframing the request in hopes of receiving an affirmative response. The good news here is that it can also be empowering, providing us with precisely the focus, attention, and energy we need for that precious (and sometimes precocious) next step.

As we "call out" our request, we simultaneously call in our recommitment to continue with the next steps of our journey. Requesting is about stating our need(s) as a way of strengthening our soul's and our body's desire to step in further and deeper.

Recall that we earlier considered the impact of chronos within the entire journey experience. In fact, the importance of articulating our need at the outset of the journeying process is often overlooked, because it may consume such a small amount of time. But it is there, the convergence of the outer call and the inner call, whether or not it constitutes sufficient duration to hold the focus of our attention.

There is something interesting here regarding the time component: most often, we don't "wait" for the response to our request. We move on ahead, having made our request – and therein lies the second of our vulnerabilities. The first, which we've already visited, is in the asking; the second is in the decision to wait or not for our request to be received and, we hope, fulfilled.

Most often we move forward, anticipating a positive outcome. Our unconscious minds are at work overtime here, always at the ready to decide if now is the moment to pause and hold off on further forward movement. Defense mechanisms may kick in at this point, based on our previous history and experience around similar quests and requests.

The Shadow Appears

Our requests can be directed toward two different sources for response. We've touched on one of the two places – an external source, whether real, imagined, hoped for, or based on faith. The other lies within: an internal "well" that contains (and retains) a treasure trove of our deepest and most intimate sources of information about ourselves, even things we don't especially want to know about.

This lesser-known, more contained, even repressed aspect of ourselves is something Jung called our "*shadow.*" As it is one of Jung's largest and most fascinating terms and concepts, let's take some time to elaborate on it here. It's a unique idea, with several aspects to its identity:

- It is innate: we are all born with it, as well as the capacity to construct our own personal shadow throughout our lifetime;

- It is universal: we can deny, repel, or even try to annihilate it, but we each have shadows that have an impact on us, on others, and on our relationships;

- It is buried in the layers of the realms of our unconscious, and is often pervasive and relentless in our dreams, our daydreams, and the things we say and do without conscious awareness;

- It is a critical aspect of our psyche that is capable of doing great harm within and beyond us, if its negative side is enacted;

- Without our or others' consciousness and attention to it, it is capable of upsetting our aspirations, dreams, hopes, and plans for the future; and,

- It is an integral aspect of all humans and the human condition.

With these characteristics foremost in our minds, we can now more specifically and positively identify what the shadow is, and how it may show up in our journeys and in various examples within the realm of the arts.

To explain the shadow fully, we must also balance it with its opposite (or its "twin"): the *persona*. The persona is our "outer self": it is the self we consciously and conscientiously cultivate and show to the world around us. Usually, it involves "putting our best foot forward." We want to be seen in a positive light, liked, respected, even admired. We are taught early on how to enhance the chances that we will be, by our parents, mentors, teachers, adult authority figures, and exemplars within our community and the world at large. Generally, this is easier said than done, and consistency is challenging: it is incredibly difficult to maintain a wholly positive persona over time and space.

The shadow, then, is the quintessential opposite of the persona. It is the darker side or sides of ourselves that we try to hide from the public – and often, even from ourselves! It is the storehouse of our negative life experiences, fears, unbidden desires, failures, hurts, pain, and suffering – and the negative narratives that we tell ourselves about all of this, whether consciously or without conscious awareness. We can be motivated to see, say, sense, and do something because our unconscious shadow overwhelms us in a given moment and takes over without our knowing. It can be that powerful.

The shadow is not always negative, but it is dark, and it can be wild and untamed, unless we've done our own "shadow work" to behold, wrestle with, and tame this other side of our personalities. Clarissa Pinkola Estes' now-classic book, *Women Who Run with the Wolves,* goes into great depth on this point. Here's a brief quote that helps to explain the concept of the shadow and our lesser known selves:

> Within every woman there is a wild and natural creature, a powerful force, filled with good instincts,

passionate creativity, and ageless knowing. Her name is *Wild Woman*, but she is an endangered species. Though the gifts of wildish nature come to us at birth, society's attempt to "civilize" us into rigid roles has plundered this treasure, and muffled deep, life-giving messages of our own souls. Without Wild Woman, we become over domesticated, fearful, uncreative, trapped.

This generates an interesting paradox for us within our multifaceted and fascinating selves. While the untamed shadow may bring us to the point of catastrophe, it may also do something completely paradoxical: if channeled appropriately, it may have a hand in contributing to a great personal breakthrough or success. This has been the case with artists who have lived on or near the edge, such as Vincent van Gogh, Wolfgang Amadeus Mozart, or Ludwig van Beethoven. The energy that can well up in us based on our storehouse of negatives is something we can get to know, and, perhaps, churn and turn into something productive.

The American Jungian psychologist and author Robert Johnson writes about "taming" and "owning" our shadows. He offers specific methods for doing this – writing in our "dream logs," using journals, engaging in pyschodrama and other therapeutic modalities – as ways of getting to know this deeper and darker part of ourselves.

As we continue to work on and develop our understanding of self in this way, he states, we can actually begin to "channel" or move ourselves out of negative shadow action and response toward utilizing the shadow for the good and betterment of ourselves and the world. We can shift the energy, the motivation, and the heightened awareness, into creativity and generativity. There is hope!

We may find ourselves bargaining with the "I/me/my" inside of us, cutting a deal to help us to step further into our journey. "If I do this (journey), I promise (myself) that I will be better able to do *x* from this point forward." Or, "In exchange for taking on this journey, I know I will be better equipped to handle *y*." Finally, there is one more variation on this theme: "If I get through this journey, I will never, ever have to deal with z again."

Regardless of the response itself, what remains important is that we can empower ourselves – like Dorothy in *The Wizard of Oz* – to seek an answer within ourselves to fulfill whatever needs or insecurities we might have. In Dorothy's case, I believe she knew her answer all along, but simply wasn't ready, or perhaps she was just slightly lacking in moral fortitude and courage to knock those red shoes of hers together thrice. Dorothy and her friends and foes will reappear throughout this book.

The critical element here is that, as we prepare to embark on any given journey, the requests that we make of ourselves, of others, and the world at large will come from both our conscious selves and other aspects about which we hold less – and perhaps very little – awareness. We have no choice but to bring all aspects of ourselves, the known and the unknown, along with us through the entire journey process.

The Known and the Unknown

If our journey is primarily physical, then the request allows us to embark with our minds alive and engaged. If the journey to be undertaken is oriented around emotional or affective growth, then our questioning may spark deeper intellectual reflection and connection. Whatever the specific emphasis of our journey experience, the request process will create a deeper level of engagement for us between many levels of duality:

- the known and unknown,

- the planned and the spontaneous,

- organization or chaos, our internalized world and the external world around us.

One other consideration about the impact of a pre-quest request is that it indicates that no one's individual journey is 100 percent scripted or predictable. Being in our questioning or requesting self means that we are not acting and thinking in the realms of smugness, arrogance, self-containment, or self-righteousness. We are actively seeking something that is beyond us, out of our full or routine control or care. For many, the request is indeed a poignant moment – a moment of letting go.

Four

⁓

The Journey Cycle, Part II: The Quest

"We're off to see the wizard, the wonderful wizard of Oz..."
~ L. Frank Baum

The Why of the Quest

As we make our requests and articulate our question(s) within our-selves or to another, we unconsciously step deeper into the main frame of our journey. Our next steps move us from "requesting" to "questing" – the longest and most strenuous part of the journey cycle. This is the "stuff" that fills books, from autobiographies to fiction and sci-fi, and is of course the stuff of so many movies.

Perhaps we know this best as the "hero's quest." It's what many of us in the US grew up with: the comic strips, Saturday morning cartoons on TV, super-heroes, our first children's books. The hero's quest was, for a lot of us, what we were schooled in – *The Odyssey*, *Robin Hood*, *Dr. Jekyll and Mr. Hyde*, Steinbeck's novels, *Star Trek*, *Star Wars*, *Harry Potter*.

The list is long, and might look extremely different for each of us. But there can be little doubt that we have been schooled in heroes – and, I hope, heroines ("sheroes") as well. No culture, ethnic group, or gender has cornered the market on such figures. They are universal, transcending time, space, and place.

Whatever else we might feel and think about this universal narrative of heroes and heroines, it seems to have become an integral part of "The American Way", although it might be more accurate to think of the hero/heroine's quest as uniting all cultures and traditions. Joseph Campbell popularized this concept in his epic book *The Hero with a Thousand Faces*.

In this book, Campbell explores the journey of the hero as s/he ventures forth from the common, ordinary world into regions of the supernatural and mystery. In these worlds, there are fabulous and fantastic forces at play and the hero, usually on a solo voyage, uses all aspects of his or her self to conquer challenges and emerge decisively, re-entering the workaday world with heightened abilities to empower colleagues, friends, and even enemies, if they choose.

For many of us, our earliest known heroes and heroines are our parents or whomever held these critical roles as guardians in our early development. They are everything to us; we are totally dependent on them. They may well have many faces until something called *object permanence* sets in and we begin to recall them time and again, without the constant fear that if they leave our sight, they are gone forever.

Object permanence is a universal phenomenon in human development. It involves the understanding that everyday objects (and people) continue to exist even when they cannot be perceived through any of our five basic senses. Accordingly, it is through touching and otherwise interacting with objects and people that infants develop object permanence.

Through his research, the Swiss psychologist Jean Piaget discovered that infants develop this internal cognitive concept around approximately eight months of age. The "empirical proof" or evidence is that they are able to develop a mental representation of the object that has just left their immediate physical presence in their own minds.

There is indeed a connection – and a strong and vital one – between object permanence and the establishment of hero figures (hero "archetypes") in a child's psyche. Only once there is some degree of trust and continuity involved can a person really develop a meaningful relationship with another. And there is a critical bridge between calling another person a personal hero (heroine) and the ongoing sense that that individual is available to support, assist, even rescue us, if necessary.

We look up to our heroes and heroines; they are models and exemplars of what we want and need and hope to be or become in some way. They are steadying elements in an ever-changing universe. Whether known or conscious or not, we bring a visual memory or image of our heroes/heroines along with us on our quests and journeys as inspirations, stabilizing forces, and models of appropriate behavior, belief, and decision-making.

Our goal in this chapter is to better understand our need for those quests. Why are we drawn to them? Let's go back to words for a brief second. What is a longer word in which the "quest" is embedded? If you responded with "question," that would be appropriate! In each and every quest, there exists at least one embedded question, and the journey then becomes the "practice" of embodying the question and the quest. Since we are not born all-knowing, the quest and the journey are not only queries in and of themselves, but also constitute our human efforts to respond.

Whether, when, and how our earlier requests receive affirmative or negative responses, we generally move forward. The questing part of any journey is what gives us the excitement, stimulation, energy, and personal power to make a go of it, come what may. While we may have an outcome in mind (as is often the case), it almost seems as if we as humans have a built-in curiosity to simply try things out, to push ourselves in some way or another. We are all basically risk-takers, depending on how we define the word "risk."

We take what we sense to be safe and move it to the next level, where there may be a hint of a doubt, a question, a wonderment – What could happen? What will happen? These are questing queries. There may be an outcome or result we desire, but we cannot and do not know what will unfold nor in the end what will transpire.

- Will something anticipated come into play and occur?
- Will there be serendipity or another kind of surprise we don't expect?
- Will a confluence of circumstances take place, with or without our knowing?
- Will something that we were anticipating not transpire?
- Will an external, independent, indirect event come into being that we had never considered or dreamed of?

All of these are potentials and possibilities, always. Perhaps it's in the not knowing that we experience excitement and stimulation – and/or fear. This stands in direct contradiction to our other, more workaday experiences that are by definition more routine and predictable.

The *What* of the Quest

The journey-quest is about action, and it is generally proactive rather than reactive. Recall, if you will, that all journeys have goals, whether specific or general. One visual metaphor is to see a journey-quest as the process of phototropism at work: like a plant bending toward the sun to maximize its intake of the sun's energies, human beings stretch forward toward their anticipated goals and outcomes of their quest.

The quest portion of our journeying is about meeting and accessing two significant elements: coping with stress, challenge, and obstacles, and reading the signs and symbols that enable us to go forward. Both happen on every quest and within every journey, often multiple times. On the quest, our skills are tested and strengthened, and our ability to perceive both ominous and hopeful signs becomes more highly refined.

While our lingering self-doubts might become restimulated or reactivated, our internal curiosity and resilience usually overcome fears and temporary paralysis. Our internal vulnerabilities – mental, psychic, soul-based, and spiritual – may come to the fore, and we may feel quite fallible. At these points, we are in metamorphosis, much like a snake shedding its skin, or a caterpillar transforming into a butterfly. In these moments, we feel naked without our typical daily protections, including Jung's concept of our "persona" which, finely honed as it is for most of us, provides safety from intrusion.

In this questing phase of our journeying, our external frailties and vulnerabilities are also exposed, and may be exacerbated by the "stretch" we are undertaking. Physical strength (or weakness), stamina, and old and newer hurts, injuries, or illnesses – any or all may be highlighted in ways that bring on fear, anxiety, and a case of nerves. But there is good news here. Remember that we each are blessed with core courage and resiliency to recover from the exposure of these vulnerabilities during this critical phase of the journey-quest.

Beyond our presenting vulnerabilities, it must also be noted that, when we are in a heightened state of awareness, we demonstrate increased feelings of stress. Stress, psychologists suggest, comes in two forms: "distress" for stressors that impact us negatively, and "eustress" as a result of heightened states of positivity from high-water benchmark moments in our lives. For example, taking on a new job brings on both, through excitement, challenge, fear, and anxiety. So, too, does the birthing of a nascent relationship, or first-time parenthood. And, of course, there's our first day of school, away from home and parents.

The continuum of diverse experiences can be scaled for each of us as "good" or "bad," "happy" or "sad." Everyone has experienced both. Each of us lives with our own broad or narrow continuum of "distress" to "eustress" through our observations and experiences.

When, as humans, we experience – or even anticipate – a stress-response (we call it "being stressed out"), we are vulnerable to yet another entirely human foible: the making of mistakes, which are unforced errors in our behaviors, interactions, utterances, and activities. These mistakes may put us at even greater risk.

Let's recall the expression, "The greater the risk, the greater the reward." Some of us may not appreciate or even like this sentiment. It's debatable whether it contains great truth (whether with a capital or small "T"), but a corollary phrase bears out here as well: "Ready or not, here I come!" No one gets through their life without taking risks, without pursuing some sort of journey or quest or journey-quest.

Jung was fond of asking, "Have you made any wonderful mistakes of late?" when referring to the chain of ongoing human behaviors. We will make mistakes, and we do fall into or create our own patterns. This is equally true in our lived, conscious life and in our dreaming life.

In Bill Murray's film, *Groundhog Day,* he is forced to live and relive the same day over and over until he comes to grips with the numerous errors of his ways and internalizes a strategy for responding differently in social and relational situations. There are countless other examples, and of course, you have your own as well. It is important that we take stock of them. Whether you know it or not, you have learned from your mistakes, and you have grown as a consequence of them.

The hope is always that making a mistake the first time will be the teacher that corrects that mistake and enables others to come forth, enabling greater learning and growth through their experience. If we fail to learn and grow from our inevitable mistakes, our journey and our quest may stall – we may become stuck in a holding pattern and lapse into a sense of stasis from which there is little escape, or hope, in any given moment.

Whether or not there is free forward movement and progression through the questing aspects of our journey, the questing element remains dynamic. It seems ironic – or perhaps even oxymoronic – that things can still be fluid and dynamic even if we are stuck. Why is this? How can we tolerate – or even comprehend – the conflict here? How can we reconcile being stuck and moving forward concurrently, in real time?

First, journeys and quests are like that. Jung refers to the "unification of opposites" – that they fit, whether contradictory or not. Becoming and remaining stuck, making mistakes, experiencing deep and surface vulnerability – all happen within a larger context of movement. All of these are experienced as "states of being" and our lives have ways of moving into, through, and beyond them. In fact, this very movement itself *is* a personal quest!

Questing through Questions

As we've noted, questing comes with questions, questioning, hoping, fearing, and the entire range of human motion and emotion enveloped and embodied within the process itself. Our ability to tolerate ambiguity, holding the one with the other, and sensing and trusting that the issues of stuckness, error-making, and being vulnerable enables us to develop greater strength, greater resources, and greater stamina to move on. Without the challenges, confrontations, and conflicts inherent in the questing part of our journeying, we would less prepared, focused, and stimulated to carry on. And carry on we do!

As we have seen, the journeyer's framing of questions while entering the questing phase is a critical component of preparation for and experience of the larger journey. Taken both individually and together, these questions provide a glimpse of the vulnerabilities, concerns, anxieties, and challenges that the journey-person anticipates upon entering the journey itself.

Questions, as we ask them, come in many forms. They may be rhetorical (not needing or requesting a specific response from another person), specific and direct (aimed at a particular person or group who may or not be present), general and indirect (to no one in particular), or personal (as a motivator or response to something in the environment or within one's self). In the broader context of a journey, questions most often are an inquiry with one or more of the following purposes:

- an inverted statement of a personal need, want, or desire (*Do I need this?*)

- an indirect (or even, very direct) way of stating an emotion accompanying an aspect of the journey (*Is this the way I want to feel now? Why am I feeling X? What will it take for me to feel Y?*)

- a clarification of information, or for communication and understanding (*Could you kindly please explain that again? Or write it down?*)

- an indirect way of stating an opinion, idea, or value (*Can I offer my opinion? Do you want to know what I'm thinking (feeling)?*)

- a way to stipulate specific conditions, circumstances, and information necessary to proceed onward with the journey/quest (*What do you need from me in order to spare my life? What if I bring or show you my "A" in order for me to receive "B" from you?*)

- a cry for help, support, assistance, or guidance (*Please, please, can you help me? Can you please show or tell me the way?*)

- a confirmation or affirmation of self, other, or both (*Did you know that I could do that?*)

Thus, there is a very clear reason why questions co-exist at the very heart of the questing aspect of every journey. Some may go unanswered from without (Job questioning God); others may be resolved from within (personal dilemmas and doubts where we rise to the occasion); and for still others – there is no clear response. Of course, the journeyer generally asks a question seeking an answer or a response. Although these words are usually considered synonyms in daily speech, in this context there is a difference between the two.

A specific answer or generalized response to a query is a statement involving specific information that is clear and focused. It often provides quantitative data that enables us to make a quick decision about a necessary action. We all want answers, even if they are not the most helpful nuggets of information in the long-term.

Answers may breed dependency – we may psychologically begin to hope for or look for information from the outside that is actually contained within. Witness Dorothy in *The Wizard of Oz* – she may well have known throughout her journey to Oz that all she had to do was tap her red shoes together three times to get home to Kansas.

Continually looking for the answers in other people may negate or at least downplay our own knowledge, power, and wisdom. In so doing, it may slow down or even paralyze us during our quest and our journey. But we should never be deterred from asking the question, whatever it is. There is great courage, strength, resilience, and truth to be gained by doing so.

A response, unlike an answer, is more of an opinion that is grounded in the experiences and understanding of the respondent. Although they may come across as fact-based, responses are more likely indicators of a direction, a way of thinking something through rather than a definitive, correct, single-minded basis for direct action. Responses are more "open-ended," whereas answers may be more "closed-ended." The framing of the question can determine whether it is one or the other:

- *Open-ended questions generating responses:*
  Why would you want to take that with you?
  How ought I best proceed?
  What tells you that I cannot accomplish this?
  If I don't sleep, how will I feel tomorrow?

- *Close-ended questions generating answers:*
  How many times have you told me this?
  Will you bring this along?
  Should I consider holding off until later?
  Where will I find it?

What did Siddhartha take with him as he journeyed out from his father's kingdom? He brought remarkably little, in terms of tangibles. What did Hansel and Gretel bring with them when they walked deep into the forest? They left behind a trail of bread crumbs. There are so many queries and responses that emanate from the realm of fairy tales that demonstrate the importance and prudence of asking questions, aloud, even if there is no one apparently present who we think might respond.

Any quester/journeyer needs both forms of questioning at their free disposal. In the asking, we undertake a deeper level of commitment to the journey, seeking wisdom, advice, support, knowledge, information, and insight in the forms of either responses or answers. As a result, we see an uptick in confidence and clarity in the ability and desire to move forward – unless the answer or response offers foreboding content.

Following the question or questions asked, there might be a moment (or more) of retrenchment, reconsideration, new planning, reprioritizing, strategizing, and so forth. In extreme circumstances, we might sometimes experience a strong and clear desire to step off the journey's path and away from the quest altogether. This might be momentary, temporary – or definitive and complete. Doing so, however, only brings us to another aspect of the journey, and not away from it entirely. Even a personal vacation – a trip or journey adventure to a new location – may be seen as a way of temporarily stepping off the Longer Journey, even though it takes on its own implications as a shorter journey!

Generally speaking, however, the more information we receive, the more comforted and confident we feel in taking the next steps. Our minds are alive and enlivened by the information we seek and receive from both the outer world and our inner world. The more things add up and make sense, the greater our state of readiness and preparation to undertake the journey. All this can only come from requesting new ideas to carry with us.

When we ask, we always anticipate receiving something in return. It is in this transition from the ask to the reception of something new and previously unknown that we move from "request" to "bequest" – the next stage or phase of the questing aspect of our journey.

FIVE

~

The Journey Cycle, Part III: The Bequest

The pendulum of the mind alternates between sense and nonsense,
not between right and wrong.

~ C. G. Jung

What Our Questions and the Responses May Tell Us

Part of the excitement – and perhaps the trepidation – of experiencing novelty, particularly in the form of a journey, is in not knowing. When we journey through our questions, we don't necessarily know two things:

- the specifics of the response or answer, and
- where, from whom, and when the response or answer will come.

Is the answer or response a gift, an expectation, or something in between? The way to think about this question has much to do with our personal and cultural values, and perhaps those of our faith or religion, if we practice one (or more) in any way. Our attitude and our degree of patience toward the response are ways of understanding our approach to the expectation/gift query.

Odysseus was gifted with the call of the sirens toward the end of his long journey. In Steinbeck's novel *Of Mice and Men*, Lennie was gifted with a mouse to care for in response to his prayers. The Little

Prince, in all his loneliness through all of his travels, received the intimacy of a fox and a rose to befriend. And, following all of his challenges during his many life journeys, Siddhartha received what he had been hoping for along: the gift of personal peace and serenity and a greater sense of equanimity within himself.

Within literature and the arts, it's not hard to find stories and renderings of journeyers receiving timely yet unexpected bequests as responses to silent prayers or enquiries spoken, sometimes shouted, sometimes through tears. When, in your own lived experience, have you been offered such gifts during your own life journey that served as surprises and offerings unanticipated or hoped for?

I would posit that we visit the full scale of the continuum from gift to expectation over the course of our questioning lives. There may be times when we are so desperate for feedback that we may feel entitled to it immediately. At other points, we may be afforded the luxury of time and space to receive whatever may be forthcoming, from whomever, whenever.

Sometimes the reception of an answer or response surprises us; sometimes it confirms or solidifies what we already know. This is about content. Our attitudes will determine for us whether we perceive an answer or a response to a question as a gift or an expected entitlement.

I recall receiving a surprise visit from a former girlfriend many years ago when I was doing my student teaching in Great Britain. I was shocked and wholly unready for this experience, and found it incredibly challenging and disruptive; yet it was a gift, and, sadly, I was unable to respond with the grace I would have wished for at that time.

Some "gifts" are not what we ask or hope for, but they arrive anyway and we must work with and through them. Has there been a time or point in your life when you were unable to receive a bequest or a gift in the way you might have wished? What were the circumstances leading up to and following this situation? What learning took place for you?

At the other end of this continuum, I can also recall many circumstances when I was able to receive the bequest of a family member, relative, friend, professional colleague, or a student. Thankfully, these are more numerous than those moments where I've felt unready or unprepared or even open to taking in an offering. What generally comes forth in these moments is genuine appreciation, humility, and sometimes, even, an unfortunate and unnecessary self-deprecating statement ("I'm not worth it"; "You shouldn't have"; "I don't deserve this…"). My goal is always to receive with grace and gratitude; it is within me to do so, and yet my own foibles sometimes make reaching this place of grace within myself difficult.

If we hold an expectation, we may well be filled with anxiety, internalized pressure, tension, and need around whatever comes to us. If we see it as more of a gift, we may feel more relaxed, at ease, and open to whatever it is we receive. Most of us have traveled across this continuum from expectation to gift over time, and when we stop to think and reflect, we will remember the distinct differences between the two.

Many of our perceptions or perspectives may be awakened, enlightened, surprised, or confirmed by whomever or whatever delivers the information pertaining to our questioning. This process is known as "The Bequest." On a questing journey, or a journey-quest, a dialogic or metaphoric response or answer to one's query is known as a "bequest" in that it is seen as a gift, an offering. We will probe more deeply in these next pages into the soulful, spiritual, psychological, and behavioral implications of the bequesting process.

The very nature of language enables the human mind to think and act in terms of dialogic "call and response." To what extent do we expect – or at least anticipate and hope for – a rejoinder to our inquiry? To a greater or lesser extent, there is a desire for input and insight from another being. Otherwise, why ask?

In the world of music, call-and-response is expected, and practiced. This form of back-and-forth is, in fact, a notable style of instrumental or vocal music. We hear birds call and respond to one another all the time – many of us think of us as "natural music." The same is true of whales, and many other species of mammals and animals. In these situations, it is a matter of communication, sometimes for survival. In most forms of human spoken communication, call-and-response is a matter of choice, will, and decorum.

As we've already considered, in the asking, we become vulnerable. If the question being asked is sincere, then we are with our best or highest selves if we are truly open to receiving whatever is given back to us, in whatever form or manner. This is what allows the response or answer to be seen as a gift or an offering – a bequest. If given, the answer or response may provide direct information or indirect clues that help to solve whatever at that moment we consider to be a "problem."

Some of us are more prone to asking insincere or indirect questions than others. This may come from a fear of being or seeming insecure, a desire not to know, feigning or masking real interest, or a bevy of other possible reasons. It may also be a cultural nuance, based on the ability, desire, or training toward directness or indirectness. We've all been there, and, deep down, we know the difference between sincerity and insincerity inside of ourselves. Journeys and questions – wherein we deliberately step outside of the comfort zone – tend to heighten the disparity between sincere and insincere, as well as the desire to really discover and know the truth, our truth.

With truth, there may be pain or suffering involved, or their opposites – joy and elation. While pain is real – often a genuine and authentic physical or emotional state – suffering is optional. Suffering comes from our telling and continually retelling ourselves a narrative that keeps us thinking or feeling in a negative way.

We do feel pain, but we don't have to feel suffering. It is often a trick of the mind and the psyche, an unconscious choice we make to hold ourselves in a stuck place. This may be a difficult concept to bring into our individual reality. Awareness to see and tell ourselves about the difference between pain and suffering is the very first step toward reducing our suffering.

Once we begin to tell ourselves (and others) a different story about what may well be painful, then we may begin, maybe, to see, feel, and hold ourselves differently. It is a very difficult thing to eliminate suffering from our lives. You might wish to take a moment here to pause and reflect, and see if this concept holds possibility for you in your life to date.

Either way, we transition from being in the role of requester to the other role as bequester. The very nature of a bequest indicates that we must actually be in a receptive state of mind in order to receive or gather in the response(s) to our question(s). No matter whether the queries or their potential answers (or responses) are life-affirming, life-threatening, or anywhere between, we must have the courage to "show up."

The US film actor and director Woody Allen claims that 90 percent of life is just about this: showing up. How, whether, and when we decide to act on the information given is an entirely separate situation. For this moment, we are more interested in "being there" to take whatever is offered in response to our questions.

Managing Ambiguity

Not every question asked by a journeyer receives a definitive answer or even a general response. And, to further complicate things along the way, what we consider to be a hard-hitting, direct question may get its inverse as a response: a reply that is perhaps obtuse, indirect, generic, or metaphoric – or, possibly, and perhaps worst of all, stony silence. We know that persistent questioning or petitioning can often test the patience of the person being asked.

If we are the questioner or petitioner, we know that it is in our best interests to formulate the best wording possible to achieve what we hope for: an affirmative response. However, in order to do so, our "questioner within" will sometimes manipulate words or the other individual involved to get what we want.

Young children – right up through their adolescence, and even sometimes beyond – are geniuses at being able to "split" their parents through persistent (some might use harsher terms like annoying, agitating, perseverating) questioning, thus taking advantage of one or the other parent, playing one off the other if necessary, to gain the upper hand and "win" their request or question.

We make our carefully thought-through and carefully scripted attempts to carry out our journey/quest plan – known as a "thesis," an idea put forward – into motion. We are then generally met with reactions, counter-plans, obstacles placed in our path, and other forms of blockage to our efforts to carry out our journey/quest smoothly, efficiently, and effectively. This is known as the "antithesis," or, more to the point, the "anti-thesis." We'll look at this in greater detail later.

It is in the midst of the thesis – and its inevitable antithesis – that the first and perhaps the most perilous period of questioning occurs. By this point, we have committed ourselves to our path, our journey, our plan. We ask questions to secure information, data, opinions, and more to help move ourselves forward. Now, in receiving the first of what will likely be many bequests tendering help or information, we have achieved a "synthesis."

Newly armed with information, wisdom, knowledge, or whatever else we have accumulated through our requests, we must decide how to recalibrate our movements, strategies, attitudes, and techniques, as well as whatever else we carry with us in order to make further forward progress along the way of our journey-quest. Of course, another option is that we may decide not to change the course of our physical or mental activities as a result of this response, answers, or silence, and proceed according to our original plan.

Thus, we are at a decision-point, which is often crucial: what do we actually do with the bequest(s) of new information from our request questions? For sure, any action on our part may receive an equal or unequal "push-back" from the universe, or by a particular person, place, or object.

At the same time, we may encounter no resistance. As autonomous individuals, many of us are free to pursue any course of action or re-action we choose, or not. Others of us may be unable or unwilling to act on the basis of what we receive – for personal, cultural, political, or other reasons.

In the event of the hero's journey or quest, we generally choose some form of action based on incoming information over no action at all. What is more complicated is receiving seemingly contradictory information from any number of sources, each indicating that their bequest of a response or answer is the most appropriate or correct one for our circumstances. Having two – or even more – apparently equal options and opportunities from which to choose is what we call a classic personal dilemma. The very nature of a dilemma is having to select from among different choices or paths in order to move ourselves forward.

Most major characters in fictional literature and motion pictures are dealing with some form of a personal dilemma – whether it be relational, intimate, professional, focused on some sort of life transition, physical, spiritual, or any combination thereof. Whether overt, subtle, or highly nuanced, each character faces one or more forks in their pathway forward through life. Sometimes there is a clear opportunity for a definitive or "closed answer" response – yes or no – and at other points the response is more of an "open answer" and must be made or reached in shades of gray. Here are a few from real life, literature, and film to consider:

- Which road did US poet Robert Frost take in his famous poem *"The Road Not Taken?"* Why?

- What options were open for the American transcendentalist philosopher-naturalist Henry David Thoreau to take in terms of paying his taxes? What did he choose to do, and why – and what was the consequence?

- Why did the lawyer Atticus Finch (played by Gregory Peck in the film adaptation) decide to defend Tom Robinson in *To Kill a Mockingbird?*

- In John Knowles' 1959 novel, *A Separate Peace,* why does Gene fight within himself and make the ultimate decision to take his own life?

- What led Ralph to break away from Jack in William Golding's 1954 novel, *Lord of the Flies?* What led up to his decision, and what were its consequences?

In all of these situations, the key or lead character faced a critical dilemma that affected not only themselves but those closest to them, and sometimes others not even known to them. On the most immediate level, each one had to make a choice and face a consequence that had not only immediate but long-term influences on a relationship, a community, a culture, and even history itself.

In this way, a bequest calls on us to make a personal judgment, a reaction to the response or answer we have been given. Let's pause here momentarily, and rewind just a bit. There is a small but critical step that is often so brief in time that we skip or ignore it. Yet, our reaction to the bequest is so entirely based on this oft-unseen moment that we may find ourselves saying, "If only…" to the step in between.

As we've seen, living and journeying fully means we are explorers in space and in time, often without knowing a particular outcome or consequence of our thoughts and our actions while in the experience of the moment. Learning that we don't know and won't know "the answer" or even a particular response to our questions means we must live in a state of at least temporary suspended animation

– otherwise known as ambiguity. Living skillfully, with grace and wisdom, is perhaps one of the most noble of the many manifestations of the "being" sense of our humanity.

Reception, Filters, and Buffers

This critical moment has to do with our reception of the information (whether with an answer or a response) given to us as we enter our journey more deeply and commit ourselves to taking in critical content. So, let's talk about filters here. A filter is a very human element in the request and bequest dialogic process. We all have them, and they are both helpful and harmful.

Our individual filters are what allow us to discern fact from fiction, truth from untruth, and wisdom from fraud. These filters are steeped in deeply cultural and familial traditions of ethics – sorting right from wrong. Sometimes our filters are really more about a question of degree – is something more good than bad, better said than done, understood more or less?

There is a degree of relativity involved in our filters. They buffer some details in and some out. We are not generally conscious of this, other than perhaps knowing intellectually that filters and buffers exist. They are idiosyncratic, and our knowledge and understanding of them is in no way equal to the power(s) they have over us.

Filters are also cultural: there are clear and sometimes strict cultural rules over what is allowed, what is not allowed, and who gets to decide. Sometimes it is the government or other institutions that give us their filters, and there is pressure and force to take them on as such. In these situations, we are often told both *what* to think, and *how* to think. There is very little – if any – autonomy, or self, in the process. These restrictions are real, and there may be severe penalties if one does not concur with or adhere to them.

The Little Prince, though young in years, is an "old soul." He is able to ask questions, of himself and others, that help him to sort the wheat from the chaff. He looks for what is real and deep and meaningful to him, and dispenses with the "small talk" that so often renders relationships little more than superficial molecules bumping into one another. In common parlance, we might say that his strongest filters are those of social and emotional intelligence. Given these assets, he is able to journey far, both externally and internally.

On the other hand, young Peter Pan is able only to filter his experience through the lens of a child unable or unwilling to grow up and grow older. His only way of seeing things maintains an innocence and lack of foresight that is so germane to children. He is, truly, the embodiment of the archetype of the "*puer aeternus*" – Jung's framing of the eternal child. In his world, we see that sometimes a singular filter is really an anti-filter in that it stifles one from seeing or living a fuller picture of the complexity and paradox inherent in the world at all times.

If we are singularly determined, we can recover the process of learning and knowing how our filters and buffers work, and what they screen in and out as we take in information and data from the external world. To the extent that we wish to reclaim the power of consciousness, our decision-making can become better and clearer. But there is no question that, for most of us in most situations, our filters and buffers are both a blessing and a curse.

While it may be easier to understand how and why our filters are positive blessings, comprehending how they may not be is a challenge. Here are a few generic examples of filters and filtering not working out well. We may miss out on a less expensive or better flight and itinerary if we decide only to purchase it from one particular vendor or airline. Or we may decide to eat something we're not used to – or not especially hungry for – but feel its effect negatively when it doesn't "go down" well. Doing something like this, whether it is against our will or through our lack of understanding, is a testimony to our need to access and utilize appropriate filters at the right moment(s). There are often stringent – even dire – consequences for not doing so.

We strain to understand the signs and symbols, the metaphors and similes, of responses and answers bequeathed to us. By default, most human beings are limited – at first – to the actions and attitudes that come most naturally to us. This is in sync with Jung's notion that our ways of knowing and doing are based on one or the other, rather than the more open and conscious one and the other.

Because of this more simplified – or perhaps simplistic – way of seeing things linearly rather than circularly, we are forced into the dilemmas identified earlier in this chapter. Were we able to adjust and modify our thinking to be on two lines or channels at once, we'd be able to think and act based on what may seems to be contradictory or paradoxical information. This is the *synthesis*, or union, of two ways of being and doing. Without this ability, we are not as good at moving forward based on both a thesis and anti-thesis at the same moment.

Bequests come as they are. Information itself in the form of response or answer, may be – or at least seem – neutral. But we imbue them instantly with meaning, value, judgment, and subjectivity. Even in periods of deep discernment, our filters and buffers may sift and bias the bequest of new information in ways that may not suit us or may confuse us. Or perhaps they are to our advantage.

To further amplify the meaning and value of filters and filtering, it is important to note that these unique and highly adaptable aspects of our humanity may appear to transform incoming data and information. This modification of new information may then appear – either erroneously or appropriately – to serve us or deny us, based on our abilities to interpret and utilize what comes forward through them.

Imagine or revisit a situation in your life when you thought you understood something in a particular way at one point, and then someone you trusted assisted you to think or act differently than your initial reaction or response. This is often seen as an "Ah-ha!"

moment, and, in that moment, we've had a reversal, a turn-around, a sudden epiphany when we engage our life through a radically different lens. Have you experienced or witnessed such a moment? Careful thought about these moments can bring enlightenment and a greater comprehension of your own deeply personal filtering mechanisms.

On a journey, during a quest, we don't know all that we will learn. Certainly, we know less in advance than we do in retrospect. The age-old saying, "Hindsight is always 20/20" (as in "perfect vision") applies here. So we generally hedge our bets, take the road that makes the most sense (and is often the most familiar) to us – for reasons both known and unknown – and carry on from there.

Since our filters and buffers carry with them such a strong sway, it is well worth understanding them more deeply. As the late Brazilian educator Paolo Freire was fond of saying, knowledge is power, and this is the same power to act and change the world. Therefore, becoming aware of why and how our filters work – effectively and efficiently – is a significant aspect of self-knowledge and any potential corrections we make throughout the many journeys we undertake during our lifetime.

The filtering we do in our lives is both life-sustaining and life-threatening. If this sounds overly dramatic to you, consider that when hearing, listening for, and responding directly to a cry of "Watch out!" or "Heads up!" with no filters on, no buffers running, means we may have the necessary time to jump out of the way of a falling brick or an oncoming truck, something we could not have seen or anticipated a millisecond sooner. Life is sustained.

With buffers or filters on, we might not have heard nor been able to heed the warning, might have heard it differently than it was intended, or might have tuned into something else far more pleasant and/or benign. In so doing, life is threatened, possibly even lost. My guess is that every reader has come across these incidents or circumstances more than once. The ability to have, use, or shut down our filters and to be able to discern the difference can make all the difference in the world.

The filters with which we live come from two sources: internal and external. Most of us are trained in and organized around the use of our filters and our buffers. Just as no two individuals are precisely alike, so, too, are all filtering agents, sets, and systems unique.

Let's explore the lesser-known of these two filter-sets, our internal filters, a bit more. In the world of psychology, internal filters are also known as self-regulators, or our ability to regulate or "normalize" our social and relational selves based on what we see and know to be most appropriate to our immediate and present circumstances. The extent to which we are able to self-regulate helps us to navigate challenging situations with grace, and, hopefully, a modicum of success.

For instance, most of us are aware that our behavior and comportment in a courtroom or at an airport should look different than when we are at home or camping or at a party. Our internal filters provide the necessary information and interpretation to correct impulsive actions or statements. Well-honed internal filters, by and of themselves, are necessary but not sufficient, however: we must be able to take action based on what they are telling us, or the filters themselves are for naught.

Our understanding and ability to work with our filters is reinforced by the social change-agents in our lives: adult, sibling, and peer caregivers and caretakers and the institutions in which we all live, work, pray, and play. We each undergo this complex reinforcement, emerging to live our lives highly trained by our unique individual circumstances. To use terms popularized by the revered Swiss educator and child developmentalist, Jean Piaget, our lives are all about accommodating and acclimatizing to the varied circumstances to which we must adapt.

I recall, many years ago, participating in a week-long Myers-Briggs Type Indicator® (MBTI) Qualifying Training through Consulting

Psychologists Press. The MBTI is a "forced choice" multiple choice questionnaire based on the work of C.G. Jung and his 1920 book, *Psychological Types*. It asks us to select our preferences among words grouped in twos or threes, and then translates our responses into a personality "type" or style across four different scales. The training required participants to pre-read a book with the brilliant title of *Gifts Differing*. I was struck by the understanding that we are born and live with differing gifts (personal strengths or assets), and we each must come to learn and perhaps re-learn, sometimes on a daily basis, what is most critical and urgent and must be attended to fully and directly, and what is not.

In essence, our individual abilities to lock onto – or block out – our personal screening mechanisms (filters, buffers, and biases) determine how we sort through and make sense of the bequests we receive as part of our journey-quest. This is precisely why no two journeys, quests, or journeyers are the same. We must apply our sharpest problem-solving, trouble-shooting, and response/reaction skills any time we are the recipients of information pertaining to a part of our journey.

This may be precisely why the American poet Robert Frost's iconic poem, *The Road Not Taken*, resonates with so many schoolchildren, and perhaps even more so for adults. I offer a small and abridged piece of it here for your consideration:

> Two roads diverged in a yellow wood,
> And sorry I could not travel both,
> And be one traveler, long I stood
> Then took the other, as just as fair,
> And having perhaps the better claim. . .

As singular beings alive within much larger familial, ethnic, cultural, and political/historical contexts, we have both the option and the opportunity to draw on all that is at our disposal, and to call on things and beings not readily apparent, to serve us in moving forward on our quest through request and bequest.

PART TWO

Six

∼

Roles and Rules in Journeying

*Where love rules, there is no will to power; and where predominates,
there love is lacking. The one is the shadow of the other.*

~ C. G. Jung

Operational Concerns: Breadth and Depth

We now turn our focus to the more technical aspects of journeying.
Having reflected earlier on both the conceptual and process-based
elements of journeying, we must now look directly at the operational
issues that are integral to every journey. Let's start off with a fairly
basic list, and then review each element in greater depth.

Relationships of the journeyer:
- To spirit-beings
- With other humans
- With flora and fauna, and the natural world
  and its elements
- To human constructs and artifacts, such
  as values, theories, beliefs, convictions, lan
  guage, thought, and attitudes

Physical considerations, including:
- Trials, tribulations, successes, and elation
  pertaining to the journey at hand

- The relative degree of cognitive and affective stability of the journeyer, including the extent of his/her flexibility
- The extent to which the journeyer is able to both "multi-task" and think and act multiplistically

The presence of mind, body, and spirit when dealing with emergencies, crises, and traumas:
- The ability to recall and draw forward parallels in life that may present themselves as variations along the journey

Cognitive/intellectual and mental state of the journeyer to:
- Draw on and utilize stored information, knowledge, and prior learning, both formal and informal
- Discern fact from fiction, and reality from fantasy
- Use one's emotional and social intelligences appropriately
- Relate past, present, and future in rational ways
- Be able to move from "received knowledge" to "constructed knowledge," as necessary and appropriate

While this is a detailed list, it is not necessarily definitive, and it is merely a working list for reference. The reader or journeyer might consider adding their own elements to this list to make it both personal and amenable to their own unique and idiosyncratic life and lifestyle. Yet, as with everything else in life, there needs to be a careful – and precarious – balance between being formulaic and being free-form.

The remainder of this chapter is intended to explore each of the elements enumerated above. As you read, please consider what works for you, what doesn't, and the relative importance of each going forward. The next phase of the journey is about to begin!

Relationships: The Critical Link in Our Connections and Connectedness

The first and perhaps most primary consideration has to do with the social, personal, and professional relationships we bring with us. No journey starts, occurs, or ends in a vacuum. Our entire relational history – each of us with our respective worlds – is in us, and surrounds us.

So often we think that by taking a trip – a journey, a quest, a sojourn, an adventure, or an expedition – we can escape the clutches of the tangible world in which we live, love, play, and work. We end up learning and knowing better. It all comes with us, no matter what.

During a journey, as individuals, we become the center of the world, our world of the journey-quest. Everyone and everything we have related to and have had relationships with becomes an unforgettable aspect of our lives. Some relationships remain integrally connected, intertwined like the bramble and the rose of traditional song. Other aspects touch, make contact and connection, then go their separate ways, still connected to and connecting with us, but not necessarily with one another. Still others have never touched, connected, or made contact with each other, but they have with us, at the center.

This is the wheel of life, uniquely ours, unlike any other ever created. This is the wheel of "all my relations." And these relations are not limited to human beings. It is so with the events, circumstances, and situations that have comprised our lives. It is so with all other sentient and non-sentient beings who have touched – and been touched by – our lives. This includes, for example, your first pet – the dog or cat or turtle at home, or the first hamster or guinea pig at school. And we have had some sort of a relational connection with the trees, rocks, and flowers that surround us. This list of our relations goes on and on.

The essential point to be made here is that these relationships are not static or stationary. Whether they can move or not, they come with us. This is why the sense of déjà vu is so fascinating and critical when it hits home within each of us.

This brings us around to our earlier discussion of *restimulation*, where someone or something reminds us of someone or something else, and we have a brief and critical reaction, whether positive or negative. This is powerful stuff. It can be both empowering and dis-empowering, in that we can discover both strength and vulnerability through restimulation. And it all comes back to relationships.

Journeying with all our relationships in tow places our quest on a continuum from "lighter" to "heavier." Think again about the back-pack and the through-hiker. We have our relations (relationships) to call on, to converse with, hold as images, to think, see, act, and feel through them. As in the bequesting aspect of the journey, the players are with us throughout.

Calling on them – dialing them up – is up to us. Which one? When? About what? What would they say? Again, we come to the important notion of perspective-taking, especially when we feel we are expe-riencing a dilemma or conundrum. Looking at our circumstances when we feel stuck, or lost, or locked in or out from somewhere or something can help move us along if we are comfortable and con-fident enough to ask for the help and support that may be available through our relationships with others.

In a sense, we are back to the concept and practice of the bequest here. Indeed, it's a very good thing that we don't always have to think, act, or feel in isolation, as insular beings. Journeying with all our rela-tions and relationships is a very personal, selective, intimate process.

Often we are the only ones who know who all those relations and relationships are, and whom we are choosing to call on – or reject. Of course, these people, experiences, pets, rocks, trees, and flowers have always been with us. We simply choose to make them conscious and known to ourselves by invoking a name, an image, a memory.

Re-introducing the Shadow

Let's look momentarily at the "other side" of journeying with our relations. This would be considered the dark, or shadow, side. Jung did a lot of deep and deeply intensive personal work and even more writing about his concept of the shadow. There is an enormous current body of literature focusing on the shadow, with new books and popular films coming out regularly that focus on aspects and stories of the shadow, making it one of the "hot themes" in contemporary psychology over the past decade or two.

The shadow is thoughtfully and appropriately named, as it describes the darker, lesser-known parts of ourselves that we often hide or sublimate, generally unconsciously – though sometimes in a deliberate, premeditated fashion as well. Because shadows are usually aspects of ourselves that we try to avoid, we are often unfamiliar with their content and their processes. An untended shadow may erupt.

Adolph Hitler is perhaps the most notorious single figure in modern human history. A few words on Hitler's shadow will speak volumes about what happens when we totally disconnect from its power.

Historical theorists have long posited that one of the (many) reasons Hitler became so hatefully anti-Semitic was because he was rejected three times by professional art schools that were run by Jews. Without dealing consciously with the sting of these multiple rejections, Hitler projected hate onto the Jewish school leaders; over time, this generalized to all Jews. When he rose to a level of unchecked power and leadership, his unconscious shadow erupted to cause what is known as the Holocaust.

Admittedly, this is a gruesome story, and most of us are familiar with its outcome. It illustrates the awesome power of the unconscious shadow to act in an unconscionable manner. Therefore, as we grow into our adult selves, we have a certain personal and societal responsibility to "come to grips" with our shadow. It is the lesser-known, perhaps less-highly evolved sense of ourselves and the hidden aspects of our personality.

When carrying our relations – and relationships – while journeying, an understanding of the shadow helps us to know who to let go of, and who not to draw on or dial up. We all carry people (and experiences, images, and things) that are actually dangerous – even toxic – to our own lives and to those around us. When we call on these during our journey, we use and even waste valuable time and energy. In such situations, calling on our shadows may likely be unhelpful to us, and may very well be harmful.

One such very famous literary example of an exemplary individual calling on their deep and dark shadow is Mr. Hyde calling on Dr. Jekyll in Robert Louis Stevenson's book, *Dr. Jekyll and Mr. Hyde*, published in 1896. As mirrored elements within one human being, the Hyde persona and Jekyll's shadow merged more and more because Hyde could neither confront nor befriend his shadow, which eventually overwhelmed his persona, with tragic consequences. This is a case of what psychologists might call co-dependence, wherein two parts of ourselves – or two people – become dependent over time on one another, and are often rendered incapable of breaking away and living or acting autonomously.

Using these shadow relations may actively hinder or sabotage our forward movement and growth. Sometimes we don't know this. At other times the hurt is delayed beyond the moment, as the poisons in our lives can be slow-moving and slow-growing. This is where the positive activities of our buffers, biases, and filters can come forth to support us and help self-correct poor choices and decisions that all of us as human beings make from time to time.

Of course, as people, we are not limited to relationships or relations only with our fellow humans. Indeed, for many of us, some of our closest connections – our most intimate forms of relating – may be with the animal, plant, spirit, or natural worlds that surround us. This is a choice we can make consciously, conscientiously, or not.

You may likely know someone who is more "at home" with trees, or dogs, or horses, or cats, or the ocean, than with people. They derive greater connection and satisfaction, or feel greater kinship and safety with other beings than with humans. Our priorities are highly idiosyncratic, and are based on so many diverse variables that it would take an entirely separate book to enumerate them!

This is why, in addition to journeying with our human relationships both directly and virtually, we must add the sum total of our connections with these other worlds of flora, fauna, and natural phenomena. These have both direct and indirect impacts on our journeys and quests. We imbue them with all sorts of meaning: seeing or chasing after rainbows is good luck; a four-leaf clover is even more so; a full moon or new moon means many things in various religions; toads are both poisonous and magical; and so on.

Let's return to our backpack analogy one final time. When you head out on any sort of trip – whether it is a physical expedition taking you to another place, or an emotional, mental, or spiritual journey that involves soul, profession, or vision – you have some power of choice over what you pack, where it goes, and what you leave behind. This is conscious, it is "above-board," and you have more or less full control over the decision. But, as we all know, we often (for some, almost always!) discover during the journey that we've left a material item behind – perhaps something as mundane as an umbrella or a flashlight. This may affect us if an experience calls on us to draw on this item – or it may not.

The same holds true for a symbolic object – a talisman, a good luck charm, a photo. And some may journey forth with a favorite and beloved animal, or hope to see a flower, pass a certain tree, hope to encounter a moment of scenic beauty. Any and all of these may be experienced as a positive omen, of good fortune going forward (the cartoon character Popeye and his can of spinach; Dick Tracy and his "magic" watch; Piggy with his broken glasses in *Lord of the Flies*). If an object is accessible but not noticed, this may be seen as portentous. Whether we carry or encounter something or someone with whom we imbue relational meaning may make a difference – small or significant – at any moment in our journey.

We shouldn't delude ourselves into believing that the success of our journey is based solely on what we deliberately bring with us. Along the way, we may find objects or beings that become critical to us, such as Dorothy collecting the Tin Man, the Lion, and the Scarecrow along with her dog, Toto, on the way to The Land of Oz.

At other times, we discard things whose purpose we cannot understand, or are perhaps contradictory or paradoxical to the nature of the journey itself, and therefore we cannot utilize optimally – much in the way that NASA rockets jettison no longer needed parts after blasting off and reaching space orbit, enabling greater speed and fuel efficiency to maintain and sustain the journey.

In journeying, we have less total control over ourselves, our lives, and our journeys than we may hope, want, or think. It is up to each one of us at every moment to align or realign with this statement of fact, and go (and hopefully flow) from there. The strength of all our relations, relationships, and connections will empower or disempower us along the path of our various journeys.

The Physical Element: Readying the Body for the Journey

The element we bring along with us that is perhaps most difficult to discern is not at all physical. And yet, this component is relentless! It is the full spectrum of our thoughts, attitudes, beliefs, values, and convictions. Separately and together, these are integral to every aspect of our journeying experiences. They are, in fact, inseparable from our journeys.

For many of us, these are our journeys. As we've already seen, many journeys are journeys of attitude, belief, and conviction. In these journeys, we may find that we never physically move to another place! Dreams are one such journey – they are personal, unique, free, and universal to all human beings. At the same time, they are not necessarily discernable or understandable. Furthermore, many dreams are not even readily accessible. Beyond this, they are certainly not controllable. If they were any of these, why would we ever have nightmares? The second half of this book, which focuses on archetypes, will provide many more opportunities to think about dreams.

Some journeys and quests require more than emotional and mental wherewithal. In fact, many of us probably consider any journey to be primarily physical in its scope and essence, with emotional and mental/intellectual considerations secondary at best.

While this, of course, is not the full picture, there may be an acute and intense physical and physiological element to some journeys. However, for some people, the very nature of a journey or quest is indeed its physical challenge. Some of us like, want, and need to challenge our physical selves and whatever the outer limits may be on our bodies. "X-treme sports" are all about this. So are the Olympics and their trials, tribulations, and triumphs.

On a continuum, the journeys at one end of the scale do not include physical elements at all. At the other end are those that are primarily about pushing our bodies to and perhaps beyond their human limits or limitations. It is a broad continuum, and each of us may select the segment where we feel most comfortable, and go from there. Others choose a place on the continuum that is least comfortable – and therefore more highly desirable.

Some of us are formulaic and quite precise about this, while others move on a sliding scale depending on need, context, content, and circumstances. It is impossible to either generalize or specify which type of journey/quest is more popular and/or more appropriate. As with people, journeys come in all sizes, shapes, flavors, and forms.

Preparation: A Critical Component

For those for whom physical challenge (and vulnerability) is paramount, emphasis must be placed on bodily preparation, protection, and awareness. One's own body potentially carries everything needed for a journey/quest of any length, proportion, and level of difficulty and challenge. The key word here is "potentially." As we all know from our unique lived experiences, witnessing, and observations, our bodies are vulnerable in one, some, or myriad ways.

In addition, our bodies may serve as assets given our physical strengths, stamina/endurance, bodily-kinesthetic awareness,and physical resilience. Whatever is enlivening in its degree of challenge is simultaneously death-defying. Here, we see examples of Jung's concept of duality and the notion of one and the other (life and death), not one *or* the other.

Even in our dreams, according to notables like Freud and Jung, our physical frailties are highlighted: our physiological issues and challenges are enhanced and focused, as with a zoom lens, to a much greater extent if our journey engages us in physical challenges and obstacles.

Of course, the more prepared, aware, and healthy our bodies are prior to a physical journey, the more robust the potential process and outcome. As an instrument of movement, progress, problem-solving, and initiation, our physical bodies serve to both move us through and extricate ourselves from the inevitable challenges, obstacles, and problems that we must face as we journey forth.

As we might expect, the process of preparation is not only mental and emotional, but physical as well. Look at the herculean task modern-day Olympians face in their quadrennial journeys: their task is to become as fit as possible for what they undertake. It is a 24/7 undertaking, to be sure.

As true as this aphorism is for many of our professions, it is not true for all. We live in an increasingly sedentary society, which has led to major chronic health issues such as obesity, heart disease, and diabetes.

We must remember that, if readiness is a state of mind, it is as much a process of preparing, protecting, and maintaining our physical selves. Like all other forms of journey preparation, it is best not done overnight – if indeed it could be done that fast. It is a huge and hugely significant step – a leap, indeed – to go from thinking and knowing about how to prepare to actually doing the grunt-work of gaining stamina, endurance, fitness, and physical fine-tuning. Building the requisite stamina takes time and daily practice.

In so doing, we must ask ourselves questions to prepare and ready ourselves, and to demonstrate our readiness to ourselves and others. No one wants to make a journey or seek through questing without having thought through their needs and priorities beforehand.

At the same time, most of us cannot afford the luxury of shutting down all of our other concurrent life processes to focus on physical preparation. As with most of life, it is about modification and balance.

- What do I need for physical comfort? Safety? Protection?
- Is this journey going to focus on and test my physical strength? Coordination? Endurance? Stamina? Dexterity? How shall I prepare for each, any, or all of these?
- In what ways must I keep my body maintained and attuned for the rigors of this journey/quest? Do I need to step up my sleep, rest, concentration, carb-loading, liquid intake?

These questions serve to enhance our physical selves for engagement in our journey, all along the way. These are not once-asked questions, but rather queries that we should ask of ourselves on a continual basis. Since, according to Einstein, energy is neither created nor destroyed, it must be used or transferred. As the transfer and use of energy occurs, we will find ourselves in need of replenishment – and then the question becomes, "Where and how do I restore my energies?" We must have a response and an answer to this question; to have nothing is not enough to persevere or to sustain ourselves.

To this question, we must have – or find – both an immediate response or answer and a contingency plan: if there is no option to rest or sleep, then what? If we have no water to slake our thirst, then what? If our one piece of rain gear is lost, destroyed, or mangled, then what? And, to generate creative answers to the physical problems that must be solved, we must have mental and physical clarity and focus.

If we lose our edge along the way, contemporary English provides us the consumptive language of food: we may feel ourselves to be cooked, fried, or baked! It is part of the fun, the challenge, and the joy of journeying to come up with in-the-moment responses and reactions to the range of challenges and obstacles, offering color, shape, dimensionality, and depth to the experience.

Journeys have an outstanding way of handing us the growth and learning that we most need, wanted or not. And because the very essence of our lives is fluid, nothing is static or status quo for long. Our hopes for sustained mental alacrity and physical focus may be just that – hopes, prayers, ideas.

Life on the road along any journey may hand us some things we didn't and couldn't anticipate, or even understand. For example, we may come into contact with a bug or a flower or a weed or a bite of food that we've never encountered, and then, *wham!* Illness, allergy, a new hurt, something else we've never experienced occurs in response. Now, we're more vulnerable than ever. How do we resolve – or simply solve – something we've never witnessed or experienced?

Happily enough we usually figure it out. Most of us have completed a journey of some sort out there in the wide, wild world. If the goal of any journey is merely to complete it, and we've done so, then, in a literal sense, at least, that journey was successful.

Usually, our goals go beyond mere completion. But completion itself is a significant accomplishment, indicative of our physical and mental preparation and our ability to problem-solve.

State of Mind: Emotional and Attitudinal Considerations for the Journey

We are all of one piece. A ubiquitous novelty song goes something like this: "… the thigh bone's connected to the hip bone, and the hip bone's connected to the back bone, and…." But it's not only the connection of our body parts to one another that makes our body tick and work relatively functionally. There's the mind, the soul, and the spirit to consider, as well.

We've already reflected deeply about the impact of our state of mind or state of being on our journey, from the moment of its conception. Readiness is as much a psychological state as a physical one – in fact, many would argue more for the former than for the latter. Suffice to say that both are critical, and both are integral to the journey in all its phases and stages.

Yet, as with the body, so the mind, too, is an interconnected instrument unto itself. Anyone who knows basic information about brain chemistry and the inner workings of the human brain would say that the brain is clearly the "trigger point" to our getting things done. We know, for example, that clinically-based depression actually slows down the neural-synaptic connection, and this in turn may cause a delay in our actions: we may appear sluggish, slow, laconic, or out-of-sync.

A healthy and vigorous mind may not be all that is necessary for an impactful and positive journey, but it certainly helps. Mental alacrity and focus as well as discerning judgment go a long way in helping us to troubleshoot and problem-solve the many obstacles and challenges that await us.

Beyond that, a healthy and vigorous mind will have space and energy for creativity and innovation. This will take us further along our journey or quest and enable us to stretch and grow, incorporating new learnings into our experience.

As an instrument, a finely tuned mind may take us in many directions, sometimes in more than one at the same time. Our ability to
work with and trust our mind encourages thoughtful and clear decision-making. This is perhaps the singular most important activity
in which we engage during a journey.

From our experience of self and our observation of others, we know
that the mind is not static. Its dynamism is centered around perhaps the most inevitable of all human experiences, and the most
challenging: change.

Our mind-sets change hundreds of times each day. We span the
gamut of emotions, too numerous to mention here. Many of us experience this continuum of emotion daily (or even more frequently
than that!), others perhaps less so. But no human being experiences
a constant, unchanging state of mind over her or his entire lifetime.

Yogis and other spiritual seekers strive for a state of constancy and
consistency, yet many question if this is a sustainable way of being
over time. It's an honorable and venerable venture, indeed – a journey
unto itself! But, while many may try, few will achieve it. If we can
stretch our convictions to take this as fact, then we also will accept
that change is constant in our lives, and that our brains are continually adapting to whatever changes are perceived or sensed.

It's important here to try not to dichotomize with our judgments of
the mind: healthy/weak, fast-thinking/delayed thinking, intelligent/
not so, and so on. The adult mind, of course, races to judgment as a
way of fitting things together like a puzzle, to respond to its perceived
need for clarity and control. Most adults endeavor to categorize all
aspects of life to help them to sort, understand, explain, and justify
them.

Children's minds don't quite work the same way. Children enter life
as experiencers, not analyzers. Because they are so fully engaged in
only this one moment, they lack the capacity, and even the interest, to
try to make abstractions such as categories based on judgment. Children will ask questions that we as adults may shudder at, thinking

them to be "inappropriate," rude, or crude. But, because youngsters are fixed only on the immediate, they don't have a judgmental perspective or sensibility to guide them. Still, as adults, we often marvel at their wisdom and worthiness for what they actually see, sense, or experience at any given moment.

The reason to try and suspend judgment about the power or other qualities of any one person's mind is that – over the course of a lifetime – one mind will experience so many ups and downs and highs and lows that it becomes hard to simply categorize a mind as simply "this" or "that." Again, we seem as human beings to need to rush to judgment at most ages and stages of our development. Doing so doesn't always support our lives.

On Balance and Equanimity

Two "states of being" are relevant to this discussion of emotional and attitudinal preparedness. As humans, we are uniquely equipped to bring them forth. There is a plethora of ways to achieve them and then maintain them, but it is no easy feat. The world, being the dynamic entity that it is, will conspire to remove them, even temporarily, from our life's trajectory.

They are, in a sense, twins, and the magic and the message of our lives may consist of learning and steadying them in the face of ongoing change, both internal and external. They are (1) *balance* and (2) *equanimity*. Let's explore each in turn.

When practiced, *balance* enhances our state of being on all levels. It steadies us and brings us a sense of internal fortitude, especially in the face of change, conflict, and personal challenge. Balance enables us to refocus our attitudinal and behavioral foci. It enables us to at least extricate ourselves from the sometimes precarious and overly emotional meanderings of our heart. Balance allows us to sort through life's vicissitudes with clarity of thought and rationality of being.

This is not to suggest that heart and feeling have no place – on the contrary, they do. It's important to factor them in, and to balance them in life's larger equation. Particularly when journeying, it is easy to lose one's self in a moment of deep feeling, of longing, of longing to belong, of perhaps wanting security and self-knowledge.

While most would say that these moments of passion are positive, even wonderful and life-giving, it is also true that passion, played out fully, can be distracting. When passionate about someone or something, we can lose our perspective on the bigger picture beyond that singular person, object, or thought. If so, we risk endangering ourselves and possibly others.

Yearning for these things can take us out of the present moment – the journey itself. Thus employing practices that help to balance oneself across several states of mind and being may be beneficial. Rebalancing brings us back to the only moment we have – the present moment. This allows our journey to continue, regardless of the kind of journey it is.

I've pushed and stretched myself to inculcate these balancing practices into my life, pursuing activation of them on a daily basis. Some examples include tai chi, meditation, physical activity and exercise, restriction of sugar intake, one-to-one time with my cat of eleven years, Mr. Max, gratitude for what I have and am, humility, and efforts to connect with, empathize, and connect deeply and meaningfully with others. I find that each of these can de-stress (as opposed to distress) me. That's why I try to practice them daily.

Equanimity takes balance one step further: it enables a certain peace of mind, a peace of being. When we seek, then touch the core and heart of equanimity, it is as though a state of grace has visited us: beyond feeling balanced, we feel centered.

According to psychologist Mihaly Csikszentmihalyi, we are in in a state of "flow" between – and beyond – boredom and anxiety. Carl Rogers labeled this notion of flow as a "peak experience"; Abraham Maslow placed it at the highest level of his universal hierarchy of needs, referring to it as "self-actualization."

This dynamic place can be as much emotional and spiritual as it is physical. Other words one might use to describe this state are blissful, transformational, transcendent, approaching and achieving wholeness, the integrated self at its highest level, being without ego, and serving as a "bodhisattva" of the earth (Sanskrit for anyone who, motivated by great compassion, has generated a spontaneous wish and a compassionate mind to attain Buddhahood for the benefit of all sentient beings).

We may touch this state momentarily, or viscerally, not even noticing it at first. Or, it may pass us by without our full consciousness of its presence. Yet, we have various practices to support us in reaching, touching, even trying to "hold" this place of equanimity. We engage with these practices as ways of centering. They may be catalysts, or at least proponents, to bring us to this balanced and centered place in our journeying. What is one, or more, of your practices in your life?

It must be noted that, however we arrive at them, stumbling or knowing, these twinned experiences of balance and equanimity are almost entirely temporary. Life's ebbs and flows, along with the evolving nature of the journey, may bring us to safety and wisdom, maybe even into the core of one or the other or both.

However, our human experience mostly bears out that we do not remain there for long. Whether along the longer journey of life or within the shorter aspects of a particular journey, balance and equanimity are not constant states of being. Rather, they should be seen as experiences in a particular moment. Acceptance of this is not easy. We want these moments to remain with us forever!

Almost all romantic and love poetry and song bring a special yearning to hold, and to be held by, such moments of balance and equanimity. This is true across languages, culture, and time. And, knowing this, we get to speak, and remind ourselves again, and again, and yet *again*, that the journey is at least as important (if not more so) *as* the (final) destination.

Pablo Neruda's poem, *"I Do Not Love You Except Because I Love You"* comes to mind:

> I do not love you except because I love you;
> I go from loving to not loving you,
> From waiting to not waiting for you
> My heart moves from cold to fire. . .

Robert Louis Stevenson's poem *"Love, What is Love"* also brings this yearning and polarity forward:

> Love – what is love? A great and aching heart;
> Wrung hands; and silence; and long despair.
> Life – what is life? Upon a moorland bare
> To see love coming and see love depart. . .

And Charles Wiles' love poem *"If Love Were Like Water"* states love and yearning in evocative images:

> If love were like water
> I'd build you a fountain
> And if love were like stone
> I'd bring you a mountain.
> If love were like air
> I'd set the whirlwinds free,
> But as these are not love
> I'll just give you me.

Using Non-"A Priori" Knowledge and Memory

In bringing our whole selves along with us in our journeying, let us not lose our minds in the process! Many in the fields of the hard sciences (including psychology) have said that our intellectual constructs – "mental knowingness" – might be the largest distinction between homo sapiens and other sentient beings within the mammal family.

Along with body, spirit, and soul – there is mind. And there are many expressions across linguistic domains that attest to the strength and tenacity of mind: "mind over matter," "never mind," "think before you act," and so on. You can probably come up with others.

Naturally, there are positives and negatives to the use of mind. It can trick and trap us into dysfunctional patterns of thinking. Therefore, the action of thought enables us to initiate and respond creatively and innovatively to problem-solve and to resolve momentary and age-old dilemmas.

Let's take a moment or two here to discuss the power of memory. Stored within us, we have the brainpower for two distinct yet interconnected storehouses: short-term and long-term memory. As we know, over the trajectory of the human lifespan, retrieval may be possible in either, or both, or neither forms: thus, there are four options all told.

In the beginning, it is thought, we have no cognizant memory: there is little to remember, at least on the conscious plane. Jung's notion of the collective unconscious openly contradicts this line of thinking. Not all who study, research, and practice in the field of psychology agree with its existence. That perspective would question, "What empirical evidence is there for the existence of a "collective unconscious"? Regardless of one's opinion, throughout our lives we all seem to have an extraordinarily challenging time recalling our earliest memories of our infancy and youngest years on a conscious and lived level.

Fast-forwarding to the other outer edge of the human lifespan, many in their elder years may have more difficulty retrieving seemingly simple aspects of yesterday: what did I have for breakfast? What did I do? Where did I go? What was I thinking? Yet, at the same time, as elders, our hold on our long-ago past may be razor-sharp and clear – sometimes disturbingly so!

We cannot underestimate the power of memory, which we bring along with us as the silent, invisible partner of our journeying. It is memory that can trigger – or paralyze – our repertoire of emotions, even before we know it: fear (fight or flight), infatuation, anxiety, delight, and so on.

So often, our responses and reactions to the data we encounter along the way are the instantaneous product of our memory. The degree of satisfaction or dissatisfaction with any one moment may be more based on its association with our past than the wholehearted aliveness of the present.

The term *a priori* denotes reasoning or knowledge that proceeds from theoretical deduction rather than from observation or experience. Of course, we can use and even enjoy this way of being as we evolve. As we grow into our thinking selves, this way of being and relating to the world comes only from the mind.

Memory translates the past through image, word, symbol, sign, or other visual or sensory constructs. These are based on our individual and unique lived observations and experiences. It is this memory that comes along with us – willingly, unwittingly, sometimes unbeknownst to us. Our reactivity or responses to data as we take it in is largely based upon our prior associations with it – such as fear, joy, ecstasy, and sadness. These are lived, rather than a priori, memories.

Our journeys engage us simultaneously in two aspects of human endeavor: past and present. When we are entirely in the current moment – without flashbacks or triggers – we are fully and wholly present. Of course, in those moments we are responding to input from within and without, but we don't have anything in our worlds or lives to relate that present moment to. We will, afterwards. But for that present moment, we are blank, open, and at least momentarily without awareness of past or precedent.

How frequent is this state of being for you? Personally, it's been a lifelong challenge for me to be and stay there. I was charmed to learn that a dear friend of mine had named her cat Present Time, knowing that saying these words would bring her into that immediate moment. Doing so, she said, coached and coaxed her into multiple daily reminders of the necessity to be and remain present to the greatest extent possible.

Otherwise, as we move – in any direction – on a journey, we may consciously or unconsciously be acting or thinking based on our past recall of (or an unconscious reaction to) similar or dissimilar events. As life is our largest and longest journey, it is composed of both past and present, and either our willingness or unreadiness to pre-flect on a particular future.

Memory is both duality and non-duality: it is give-and-take, yin and yang, and the entire set of opposites that present themselves throughout the course of our lives. And yet, it is not, in Jung's own words, a question of one or the other – rather, it is how we can learn to integrate one and the other into the patterns of our life, behavior, and thought.

The baggage of memory can propel us forward and catalyze growth, activity, and our own human evolution and revolution. Or, it can stagger us, paralyzing and stymying us into stupefaction and numbness, the classic deer in the headlights phenomenon. All are possible, all are human – and every one of us has lived the full gamut of this diverse range of experience.

Along the journey, we are constantly referring to what's in front of or beside us by drawing upon our past history and making parallels with it. It's uncanny. We do this whether or not we are aware of it. We are always making judgments, large and small, about ourselves, about our past, and about how all of this relates to this moment in the present. We cannot evade or avoid this. At the same time, so much of it happens unconsciously, sometimes we cannot bring awareness of this behavior into our present consciousness.

Even if we say we are traveling lightly, it is still wise and prudent to be aware that this baggage inevitably comes along with us. What we make of it, of course, is another story entirely. But, be assured: our past is with us in our present!

We are generating our own knowledge, understanding, and "agreements" within ourselves and the outer world as we enter, pass through, and exit every journey we undertake. One of the best books I've read about knowledge creation is *Women's Ways of Knowing*. This book was written by four female academics, including one of my earliest mentors, Jill Mattuck Tarule, in 1986. While covering its topic in depth, it has a rich yet simple synopsis. Its basic and overarching premise is that we (not only women, but all of humanity) transform ourselves over the course of our lives and our journeys from silence and received knowers (taking in the world as it is presented by others) to constructed knowers (generating our own theories and knowledge through theory, practice, observation, and experience).

For those of us who have traveled – journeyed – outside our unique zones (or thresholds) of comfort, we are continually in a place of not knowing. In being there, we have to create based on the combination of past and present, or of received and constructed knowing. This is part of the thrill of any journey. It is the changing admixture of the known and the unknown, the expected and the unanticipated, with facts that don't (or may not) add up, and the multiple, ongoing asymmetries of life.

As we grow and develop through the process of individuation, we become more familiar with and trusting of the notion of "not knowing" and the unknown. In our adulthood, we may use this known sense of the unknown to our advantage, and find ways to redefine it at particular moments from a new perspective, and in different terms, including "curiosity," "adventure," "mystery," "fork in the road," and so on.

As we move on in our lives, we learn that it is our attitude, at least equally with our behavior, that marks the way things can and will play out in our lives and on our journeys. Learning to gain and maintain an attitude of equanimity, balancing prior knowledge with what we both know we don't know and don't know we don't know, can help us to maintain our sanity, stability, humility, and the critical search for support and guidance.

SEVEN

~

Journeying and Human Identity

We have come nearly full circle in our exploration of journeying. We've explored particular foci that emerge as we consider the internal and external journeys we take throughout our lifetimes. In addition, we have examined questions, content, and context, all within a "unique-to-universal" continuum, including the following elements:

Unique → *Idiosyncratic* → *Cultural* → *Universal*

In this chapter, we will focus our attention on the largest – and the most abstract – component in this continuum, and reflect on that which is universal with regard to the journey. In so doing, we will attempt to transcend cultural, linguistic, racial, class, religious, and other classifications and categorizations pertaining to the human experience.

Are There ANY Human Universals?

I've often enquired of my students at all levels whether there is any singular aspect of human existence that may be classified as "universal" – that which is experienced, understood, or agreed upon by all without exception. This question has been debated hotly for three-plus decades by scores of undergraduate and graduates in my classes and courses, and likely for centuries elsewhere.

I watch, and wait, and listen, responding to questions, protestations, triggers, personal anecdotes, and the like. Students can be passionate, persuasive, and convincing. They also can challenge one another, sometimes more adroitly than I might. Listening and reflecting have served me well in these discussions. So far, nothing but birth (life) and death has secured the accord of all constituents as inevitable and universal.

I'd like to add one more item that has yet to be raised by my students: the journey of life itself! No matter what it looks or feels like, no matter how one expresses or responds or reacts, there is a journey between those two poles, no matter how short or long. As long as we are alive – and, many think, beyond life itself – we are in it.

As such, journeying is a universal human experience. We may call it many other things, as faiths and languages and cultures do. But, insofar as we each evolve, grow, and develop as human beings, internally and externally, we are in the journey of life. But what does this actually mean, and what does it actually involve?

Let's pause, briefly, to deconstruct what life and living actually involve, daily and minutely. To do so is to search for universals, hidden in plain sight or less apparent. In the physical sphere, we breathe, we react to stimuli in our sensory fields, our hearts beat. We may perspire, we digest food and process water, and most of us move our bodies. Intellectually, according to René Descartes, "je pense, donc je suis" ("I think, therefore I am") – and thus, conscious thought is a part of virtually every human being's experience.

We express ourselves within a diverse range of different iterations – verbal, nonverbal, bodily/kinesthetic, artistic, musical, prayer, and more. And we are social animals, as well: few of us grow up in an absolute bubble or vacuum. We need the help, advice, support, and guidance of others to survive, much less thrive.

The Starting Point of Our Stories: Birth

Life's journey has one basic, inevitable entry point: birth. Today, more than ever before in human history, there are multiple ways of getting there. But there is no escaping birth if one is to have a life. Of course, any birthing process is fraught with peril, or the potential for it, and many, many things must go right to enable one's birth to be successful.

Merely getting to the point where life successfully follows birth is itself a journey. It typically involves another person (or two) to be engaged in bringing the birth to reality. Often it includes more than one person, even a system or institution, a procedure or multiple procedures.

Birth may have become routine in certain societies and cultures – but it is never simple. And in many places in our world, it still entails substantial risk – of infection, of disease, of mishandling, of (gender or other) bias, of issues in utero, of bodily malfunction of infant or mother. The list of considerations is long and challenging. We can never presume a smooth birth process and a healthy baby in advance. So, there is a universal start-up in the journey of life. Yet no two births are the same; there is always a momentary or unique aspect or twist or distinction to be made, even with the birth of identical twins.

But there can be no doubt that there is a journey of arrival. And there are several ways that stories may be told to announce this arrival: photos, cards, videos, calls, emails – we take, do, hold, and memorialize them for the remainder of our and our children's lives. Sometimes they become highly public or publicized events. Occasionally, no one is present to record them, and this great moment of transition into the human family may be lost over time. I've met people from other countries who simply do not recall and have no proof of their actual date of birth. But there is no denying this huge aspect of each of our Big Journeys.

I could push on here and suggest that, with this arrival, there is usually some form of human – and generally humane – ritual. These are rites of passage created to acknowledge, recognize, and celebrate the successful completion of birth and entrance into the outer world that the newcomer then becomes socialized and acclimatized into. Is this true for you? For your children? For those around you?

These rituals may not take place in the moments immediately following a birth, but generally occur soon thereafter. Sometimes it's a naming ritual, for example, like the one that occurs in many Native American clans and families, or a religious or faith-based ritual, such as a Catholic confirmation or Jewish bris, or simply friends bringing meals to the new parents.

The specifics of these experiences are clearly not universal, but the idea that there be something done to acknowledge a new arrival into the human family may be. Generally, there is appreciation from one or more adults that a baby has been successfully birthed. Sadly, this emotion is not universally shared; those cultures and families wherein happiness is not a common feeling are well known in the literature and the world.

For example, many oppressed minorities – for examples, the Hazaras of Quetta, in Pakistan, or Palestinians in Gaza, and many others – wake up every day knowing they are hunted and hated by those in power over them. In addition, it was not so long ago that China had a law allowing most families to have only one child, and with males being more highly valued than females, the infanticide of girls was widespread. As such, the birth of a girl was all too often looked on with disdain.

In the US, a relatively recent highly regarded Broadway show, *A Chorus Line*, echoes just such a sentiment. One of the characters states, "I was born to save their marriage, but when my father came to pick my mother up at the hospital, he said, "Well, I thought this was going to help, but I guess it's not." Universals get a little murky in this area – but are still worthy of reflection and consideration.

As we've said, any journey begins with one step – one moment, one hour, one day – at a time. It cannot be otherwise. It is especially apparent at the birth end of the life-journey that life and any journey happens one breath at a time. We may become so entangled or confused or overwhelmed with the larger arc of an activity due to our future orientation that we lose sight of this necessary deconstruction: one step, one breath at a time. This simple observation is also quite profound.

Without each of these elemental processes, in virtually each and every moment of our entire existence, there can be no movement in any direction! Like birth, this is a human universal, and together, breath and movement form the very most basic element of every human narrative. Movement and breath allow for life's journey beyond the womb to inch forward; thus, the journey within and beyond begins.

The Role and the Archetype of Death in the Lifespan

Are we the only living species that is aware from early in our lives that we all will come to meet the other end of life's continuum, that of death? Of course, some will not agree that death is the end – they may see it as merely a transition into another form. But it is about the awareness that I am speaking of here: we know, in advance, that this will happen. It is conscious, and the foreknowledge of death may in fact be responsible for many of our actions: greed, impetuousness, materialism – all part of a "do it now, one never knows" approach to life.

Most cultures, religions, faiths, and families have ways of marking and demarcating death and its approach through various rituals, ceremonies, rites of passage, even celebrations. Yet, many of us do whatever we can to avoid or ward off death, in spite of our awareness of its inevitability. There is generally joy and excitement concerning birth, and sadness and fear regarding death. A huge and growing literature focuses solely on death as a core element of human life.

We learn and we do what we can to make a good life for ourselves and to provide a good life for others, although there is no universal agreement on what this looks like. Although pain, and even suffering, are part of this equation, most of us do what we can to enjoy what there is to enjoy, as we are able and allowed (or allow ourselves) to do.

That death exists in life may be what imbues it with greater meaning – nothing is forever, and we must make choices and decisions knowing or at least considering this. Thus in each aspect of life is embedded its opposite. This is the yin/yang duality at work again.

As a collective and universal archetype, death and dying represent many things for all of us: change, an end-point, bodily decomposition, the end of human awareness and consciousness, and, of course, the cessation of all previous human activity and endeavor, along with a link between past, present, and future, and often the engagement of some form of ritual demarcation. For some, it may also symbolize a (new) starting point, a celebration (of life) that may include feasting, dancing, singing, storytelling, and decoration.

For some faith traditions, death is indeed a beginning, a transition from one sentient form of being into another, and a step toward greater enlightenment. For others, it is a finite point, a surcease of all that is and was connected to that person's physical being, and it brings with it a strong sense of ending, mourning, grieving, and sadness.

We can simply note that all the emotions, activities, and attitudes regarding death are an integral part of the human race and experience. They play out in unique ways according to one's personal, familial, and cultural values. There is "big death," on the macro level – universal, known, with many consciously known features. And there is the "micro death" of one individual, evoking all sorts of idiosyncratic features based on religion/faith, socioeconomic class, gender, culture, and so many more variables.

As with all archetypes, death imbues life with greater and deeper meaning. Perhaps this seems paradoxical on the surface: how can an event demarcating the end of life as we know it add more to life itself?

From an archetypal perspective, there is, in everything, the specter of its opposite. Some would consider this to be "yin/yang" duality in motion. Without darkness, there is no light; without night, there is no day, and so on. What gives meaning and depth and perhaps urgency to life is the foreknowledge that we are here as humans for only a very short time, and we should value and treasure that time, as it is precious. Death holds great meaning to us because life itself is meaningful, and the process of dying into death is profound as well.

Whether we celebrate or mourn, sit in sorrow or in peace, hold any form of ritual or rite of passage, we are aware of the power and influence that death has, both individually and collectively. In "Turn, Turn, Turn," a 1965 hit song by the US rock group The Byrds, using a passage from the Bible [Ecclesiastes 3:1-8] and set to music by Pete Seeger in the 1950s, we hear an evocation of this rich range of experience around the universal phenomenon:

> To everything, there is a season,
> And a time to every purpose, under heaven.
> A time to be born, a time to die,
> A time to plant, a time to reap,
> A time to kill, a time to heal,
> A time to laugh, a time to weep...

For Jung, death is yet another poignant example of what he called "the unification of opposites": here, the two polarized dimensions of birth and death come together to form one constant and universal continuum: life itself, in all its transient forms.

Our Stories, Others' Stories

In any one person's life narrative, these universal experiences are embedded and intertwined throughout the course of their life. Each story is unique, to be sure: no two beings travel the same path 100 percent of the time, not even if they are a twin, or conjoined.

The way The World, writ large, responds to each individual being is similarly unique. It cannot be replicated, no matter what we may try to experience, simulate, or stimulate. Does this argument hold for you at this point? Let's go a little deeper in case you're not yet convinced.

One basic modality of universal human communication is storytelling. We learn and live (both directly and vicariously) through our own and one another's stories. In them, we see ourselves, or aspects of ourselves – sometimes happily, sometimes not.

Recently, I was asked to eulogize a dear friend of many decades. I gave deep thought and gravitas as to what to share, and how to share. I came up with images, all of which were attached to personal stories – and those threads became a narrative.

But then I stopped. I held my stories and my perceptions of my friend's life-journey in abeyance long enough to recognize that, to the hundreds who had gathered to pay their respects, to celebrate and memorialize our friend's life, we each had our own personal narratives of her journey. They were unique to each individual, and yet we held them in common.

So instead of telling my own stories, I asked that we hold a minute of silence in order that each of us could bring forth our own stories, our individual narratives, and how our friend deepened and enriched each of our lives. Doing this in silence and the solitude of our own images and memories was a deep, powerful, and poignant experience for many who participated.

That is the making of a life. It is in the stories we tell, the stories we hear, and the stories we share. They form a universal story – the journey of a life, of a lifetime. In our minute of silence, we each went "inside" to commemorate our unique and individual stories and journeys with our deceased family member/friend/partner/colleague.

This was a powerful and haunting moment of recognition for me. I had a hint here of a human universal: the journey and the unique ways that we each recall, remember, reflect upon, and express it.

This, I believe, is a universal aspect of our human existence. Where are you with regard to this information now? Has anything shifted within you as you read and contemplated this?

The Human Myth

Everything beyond our basic beginning and ending is our individual, highly idiosyncratic story, unfolding in very small units over time. This is our personal Journey, which appears at a macro level for us, and at a micro level for the world at large. Living the story, of course, is steeped in our perceptions of self, others, and the world.

Our attitudes, values, beliefs, convictions, and, most outwardly, our actions and behaviors give shape, depth, volume, and form to the Big Journey and all of the millions of journeys within it. Recall that the American philosopher Joseph Campbell, a contemporary of C.G. Jung, often asked, "Where are you in your myth?" I've always found this to be a breath-stopping question, and a refreshing one at that. It's a wonderful query to consider: life as journey, life as myth. Life is something even larger than itself, if it is considered "mythic"!

But what is myth? This is actually a highly complex, stylized question that has engendered tremendous research across cultures and history. To give this topic the in-depth attention it deserves is beyond the content and context of this book. Suffice to say, for the moment, that myth is a traditional story, especially one concerning the early or ancient history of a people or explaining some natural or social phenomenon, and occasionally involving supernatural beings or events.

For our purposes here, we can say that myth is the human creation and depiction of lives and events pitched at an archetypal level. For the moment, suffice to say that archetypes represent personal characteristics, ways of behaving, images, or symbols that are universally recognizable. Although we all may share a common understanding of each archetype, we also each have a personal relationship with them, which is influenced by many factors from our conscious and unconscious life experiences. Myth takes life and extrapolates its arc into terms and events that we can all recognize and find parts of ourselves within. It takes the form of story, narrative, a re-telling of the broader human experience. The second part of this book will pursue this idea vigorously, in greater depth and detail.

We create our own stories, our own myths, through the millions of decisions and happenstances that occur over the course of our lifetime. And we've found so many ways to record, recall, detail, express, and articulate them for the benefit of ourselves and others. We are each uniquely equipped to find modes of expressing and sharing the journeys within and across our lives, from the very basic and concrete (the wail of a baby) to the very complex and abstract (art in all its forms).

Along the way of the Big Journey (life itself), many cultural milestones take place as a matter of course and our membership in the human family. Many of these are journeys in and of themselves – rituals, rites of passage, transitions – that have been honed and honored, perhaps altered over time. For example, the questions below contrast the differences in rituals from the United States of just a generation or two ago, and heading forward into the next generation:

- What is the relative importance and relevance of high school proms?

- How often do young men ask a young woman's father for her hand in marriage?

- Are places of faith and religion as well attended now as in the past?

We all have our stories to tell about these, and related, life events. They may be highly publicized or highly private, intimate, or personal – in fact, no one else may know about them. But perhaps the very fact that life moments like these take place is universal. The specifics of each of them fall somewhere on the continuum from unique to universal depicted earlier.

Conceptualizing, Practicing, and Accepting Change

Yet, life as a process, with its twinned experiences of birth and death at each pole, is rarely so simple and stark. We pondered earlier about the phrase that Jung was fond of saying, "It is not a matter of one or the other, but, rather, how we can come to accept one and the other." I would add to this by pluralizing "other" to connote that there are many "others" beyond the stark black and white many of us come to see and blandly accept as the "all" of life.

There's so much gray in between: sometimes seen, mostly overlooked. But the gray is there, and our language has so many ways to express its conditionality: *maybe, sometimes, should, could, possibly, it depends*, and so on. How we live our lives has much to do with how adept we become at recognizing constantly changing circumstances. In addition, we must also factor in the extent to which we can shift and adapt ourselves to the constant flow of change, even when it is least expected.

In my various professional roles – as teacher, professor, administrator, counselor, mentor, trainer, facilitator, therapist, group leader, and always as fellow human being – I've noticed that there is one thing among all others that colors and gives shape, breadth, depth, and form to our lives: our responses to change. Change, like time, has an entire vocabulary dedicated to it: *management, control, frustration, fear, stress, minimize/maximize, optimize, prioritize, limit, access, desirable/ undesirable, embrace, negotiate* – you could probably add more words to the list.

Change is a constant part of our identity, an ongoing element that accompanies us at every moment. We can fight it or go with it, or even let go of it. All of us go in one or more of these directions throughout our lives. In fact, if nothing else, all journeys have as their primary focus change and our ability to adapt and modify ourselves to the dynamism of life.

Movement: Within and Beyond

The Vietnamese Buddhist monk and Nobel Peace Prize winner Thich Nhat Hanh says, "Peace is every step." In each of those steps, change (of perspective, understanding, balance, equanimity, attitude) is current and present, whether or not it is accounted for. The journey of ten thousand miles begins with the first step, and we take one step at a time to get to and go from there. The variables as we step forward, into, and through our journeys are many, and how we view and address them is in itself the first step: then it's time to move forward. In songwriter David Mallett's *The Garden Song*, the first line indicates a journey's beginning:

Inch by inch, and row by row, gonna make this garden grow...

In each step (or phase or stage) of every journey, there is a universal factor: movement. This motion and action may – or may not – be overtly physical. It may be movement of thought, an act of spoken word, a vision. What unites each and all of these? Change: something has shifted from where it was in a previous moment or iteration.

Whether change is perceptible to others who are not directly engaged is a legitimate question. But, to the individual questor or journeyer, it is somehow known, sensed, felt, tangible, and attributable. There is movement, and the journeyer moves on. The next step in the journey is underway, and everything now has changed.

Let me offer a physical and tangible example out of my own journey book. This is the overnight, there-and-back hike up and down the South Rim of the Grand Canyon in Arizona I described in Chapter Two. With every step going down the South Kaibab Trail and back up the Bright Angel Trail, I experienced multiple changes and movements:

1. I was in perpetual motion as a physical entity
2. I needed to take a breath with each step

3. The view changed, much like a 3-D color postcard when it is moved even a fraction of an inch (as with a hologram)
4. I perceived that my space and time had changed accordingly
5. I was progressing in my journey and had a finer understanding of the challenges and obstacles still facing me
6. I was one step closer to the ultimate goal (reaching trail's end)

With certain journeys, our understanding and awareness of self, other, and world are similarly enhanced and enriched by our every step and process. Journeying itself is an inherent and universal aspect of our human identity, just as are birth and death. I believe that this fact has the potential to unify us, beyond the scope of our differences.

PART THREE

EIGHT

~

The Place and Play of Archetypes

*What you leave behind is not what is
engraved in stone monuments,
but what is woven into the lives of others. . .*
~ Pericles

Framing a Definition

As we continue along this journey together, we make and mark a transition: it's time to introduce Jung's increasingly popular concept of "archetypes." In Part Three, we'll find and experience definitions of archetypes, examples of archetypes, archetypal patterns, the personality of archetypes, and how they factor into and influence our journeys, our experiences, our lives, and our relationships. Let's start with some beginning images, to help envision and visualize archetypes as a concept and entity.

Imagine our backpack at the start of a journey: it's empty. It can be filled, potentially, with any number of items – supplies, materials, and other things. Some compartments of the pack may be left lighter or empty, to be filled along the way, while others are stuffed to bursting. It's not random: after all, we packed it deliberately, selecting what was most appropriate and what we'd need and use for a specific experience. Try to hold this image as we delve into the play and place of archetypes in this chapter. You may find yourself taking along some of what's shared here, discarding some, and juggling things as you sort through your options and opportunities.

Jung said that "there are as many archetypes as there are situations in life." Doesn't that mean limitless, endless, unpredictable, and even unknowable? Indeed! So – that's our starting place. And yet, there's more to it than that. It's not only unknown and without limit – archetypes are also discoverable, they are tangible, and they have patterns: we enter them as they enter us. Archetypes are real elements of ourselves, our personalities, our identities, and our human activities and experiences.

Here's another image. Think for a moment like an architect or an engineer. To construct something, you must first have a blueprint of it: a drawing, not to scale, but detailed enough that you or anyone in your professional domain could interpret it and come up with different schemes to build something that would be consistent with its mapping on paper.

This blueprint will have symbols, numbers, letters, lines, arrows, and many other ways of communicating information that can be understood and appreciated across time, culture, and language. It represents breadth, depth, space, and dimensionality. It can then be translated, in real time, into experience. To do so, one needs the appropriate tools, supplies, materials, time, energy, creativity, and intelligence – and perhaps some help from others along the way.

With the right supports, in time, this blueprint can morph from a two-dimensional drawing (quite complex in and of itself) into the desired three-dimensional object. It is the same when members of the human or flora or fauna families enact archetypes during the course of their lived and known lives.

The one difference between a built object and the life of a sentient being is, essentially, one of autonomy: beings have some degree of autonomy, or the right to choose, decide, select, and act, while the vast majority of constructed objects do not.

Thus, a 3-D breathing being is infinitely more complex – and prone to change – than any human artifact (although computer geeks might not agree!). As we try out, take on, reject, or change particular archetypes, much within us – our personalities, values, complexes, attitudes, behaviors, aspirations – may shift as well.

Here's a third and final image to consider at the moment. Imagine you're an athlete, holding a ball – round and filled with some material (air, cloth, water, rubber bands, string, tiny pellets, whatever). You're grasping something that has all the elements of any three-dimensional object: height, width, depth, weight, size, volume, and shape. And you're able to move or transport it from Point A to Point B, more or less at will.

Now imagine that you pass it on to a friend or teammate. Suddenly, in taking this ball, they re-create it in their own likeness, with some of its core elements changed into something that they can call their own. It's changed, but its essence is the same: it is still a ball – it rolls, moves, can be thrown or kicked or hit or bounced, and in addition to being transported any number of ways, it can again be caught or held or grasped by someone else.

This is an analogue of an archetype: it retains and maintains its core elemental being, but may be "interpreted" by each person in a slightly different way. Individuals may "personalize" or tailor their ball to fit their own observations and experiences. The extent or degree of their comfort and familiarity or ease is not directly related to their skill or aptitude with that ball. Rather, it is made based on their conscious (and perhaps unconscious) experience and knowledge.

The "What" and "It" of Archetypes

What is especially challenging as we grapple with and hope to grasp the "it" of archetypes is that we must make a transition in our understanding of things from dualistic (either/or, black/white) to multiplistic or pluralistic. Archetypes work or play out in our lives, or in life in general, in more than just one or two ways. If you believe there is beauty in diversity, then archetypes hold unfathomable elegance. This will unfold as we peel off layers of definition, understanding, and experience.

Archetypes arise out of what Jung called the "cesspool" of our unconscious, or the *collective unconscious.* This is perhaps an unfortunate term, pairing one rather unwelcome and unsightly image with another that is far less understood. What Jung meant by this is that over the long arc of history, the evolution of culture includes all of our personal and idiosyncratic images, memories, dreams, and nightmares. In essence, they have become "pooled" over time to form one large mass of shared understanding in all of our unconscious minds.

Archetypes represent personal characteristics, ways of behaving, images or symbols that are universally recognizable. Although a common understanding exists, we all have a personal relationship with each archetype. This is influenced by many factors from our life experience.

Although highly controversial, and without any hard-core empirical evidence, Jung and his followers to the present day are convinced that there indeed *is* a "collective unconscious." In addition, their further understanding is that we, as individuals, draw on this collective unconscious in our dreaming and waking lives, and are highly influenced and affected by it and its innumerable components.

Jung noted that these elements rise up in all of us. For him, the collective unconscious is a universal aspect of human existence. Jung believed that there was one race – the human race – and that we share and hold as much in our unconscious as we do in our consciousness. Much as our human genomes, including our RNA and DNA, exist in all people, so too do archetypes, as they constitute an integral component of our unconscious selves.

It might not surprise you to know that at the time of his conception and writing of these terms, there was much controversy. Critics argued that there was no empirical evidence or concrete proof of their existence, and Jung had a difficult challenge ahead of him to convince his skeptics of their validity. Even today, mainstream Introductory Psychology textbooks and courses give him little mention. Using his clients' dreams, drawings, and his own lived experiences, and observing others and paranormal phenomena, over time Jung built a strong case for the existence of these concepts and their integrated realities.

Our personal unconscious, and then our personal consciousness, "activate" the backpacks, blueprints, or balls that were introduced earlier. We complete and activate them from the more general, based on collective human experience over time, place, and space, to the more specific and particular. This unique activation is based on our individual and nuanced life experiences.

In fact, archetypes form, shift, and deepen over time. As an integral element in the collective unconscious, they evolve over the course of human history, and are translated from the collective unconscious into the personal unconscious and finally to personal consciousness over the arc of our individual and unique lives. We may get to know them better – or try to retreat or retract or avoid them – but they remain. Thus, they are an integral part of the totality of our existence and life experience.

We engage and interact with these archetypes. We are in ongoing relationship with many of them, whether we play, fight, work with, or try to evade them. There is some form of active verb that we each utilize to describe or identify our connection with (or our disconnection from) each of them. We will discuss examples in this third part of *Journeying with Your Archetypes*.

Above all, archetypes are nothing if not flexible, dynamic, and evolving. For those who prefer or need a set way of seeing and doing things, this fluidity can be a challenge. We are not speaking of a fixed, static, and finely finished factoid or product here. Like many other lifelong processes, the concept of the archetype is one of multiplicity and dynamism.

Furthermore, every individual perceives archetypes and archetypal patterns differently than every other individual. For this reason, we must look to generalized images of archetypes to perceive and evoke the vast array of possibilities before moving on to particulars.

What shapes our unique understanding of this concept of archetypes, and our ability to grasp and refine our comprehension of it? Let's look at some of the key components that give shape, form, and life to embracing an archetypal approach, with all its patterns and elements. Here, we are focusing on the big issues – even existential considerations – that are at the core of forming our personal identities, cultures, and communities:

- Values (including beliefs, convictions, faith and religion)

- Ethics (codes of thought and action that shape our behaviors, actions, and attitudes)

- Priorities (in terms of lifestyles, life choices, and preferences)

- Collective cultural/historical/heritage events and experiences (including rituals, rites of passage, taboos, celebrations, commemorations, holidays, and holy days)

At their broadest level, archetypes have universal qualities. They exist across culture and time as generalized entities representing the totality of human experience. We give them names and identities, in the form of nouns and verbs. We do this to express them through image and word in ways we each identify (and identify with). In so doing, we engage with them in more personal terms, through our lived observations and experiences.

One need only look to the tarot – and the major arcana in particular – to grasp some of the more "popular" or well-known archetypes: the fool, the clown, the trickster, the hero/heroine, the lover, the king/queen/ prince/princess, the eternal child, teacher, visionary, hermit, explorer, beggar, peacemaker, father, mother, crone. A small and random sampling of other archetypes could include passion, birth, death, the desert, mountains, rivers, oceans, marriage, sickness, pain, and joy.

Surely, these exist and have their parallels across cultures and time in recorded human history. At the same time, they transcend individual cultures and are reborn and recreated within them. We need to hold and cherish this duality – it's not a contradiction nor is it a paradox – as we proceed.

One potent and poignant example is that of the Great Mother. In terms of the collective unconscious, we may be speaking more indirectly of Mother Earth, something almost of us can identify with, although the look of it is different and unique depending on where on Mother Earth we are born. Let's trace this particular archetype as one example, moving through Jung's three layers of human awareness.

In Jung's vision of the collective unconscious, the Great Mother is that entity or being from which we all – the entire human race – have evolved. According to Jung, it is embedded in our unconscious. As such, it does exist, although in this iteration it is formless and indescribable. However, upon birth into the outer world of other beings, we come into personal contact with our specific birth mother, or the adult guardian who raises us.

In making this shift from the collective to the personal, we move from the collective unconscious to the *personal unconscious*. We are now able to become wired into our own birth mother, and the developmental process through which we begin to recognize her and know she is with us even when gone (knowing she will return) is, as you'll recall, known as *object permanence*.

As we grow, especially in relationship to our birth mother or guardian mother, this archetype becomes raised to the level of *personal consciousness*. Now, we begin to have and give our mother her own shape, form, name, personality, characteristics, and unique quirkiness. The Great Mother has now come full force into our active daily lives from the collective to the personal unconscious, and then into our personal consciousness. This is how it works in Jung's system with all archetypes.

The Place of Archetypes in Our Lives

Archetypes serve many functions for us in our human, ordinary and yet extraordinary lives. They are "grounding forces" in the immediate present that help anchor us during the ups and downs of our daily experiences. They are catalysts that help us to dream and envision our futures that are both unknown and unknowable.

As such, archetypes may bring to us a clearer understanding of our heritage, our culture, our identities, of a time and people that we've never met in our daily endeavors. Looking at this from a bird's eye view, archetypes transcend chronos – time – in that they enable us to hold a concurrent past/present/future orientation as they come into greater focus in our lives, our psyche, and our soul.

As individuals with unique personalities, humors, temperaments, and multiple other aspects of our self-hoods, we do not all experience each and every archetype. This is simply not possible. As each human being is unique, so, too, is their experience of and relationship with each archetype.

However, we can learn to understand, appreciate, and even tolerate a far wider range of archetypes, archetypal images, and the archetypal underpinnings of life's events and experiences even if we do not experience them directly. In other words, we can expand the observations and experiences in our lives and world to include things that we experience vicariously, through others or through indirect experience such as literature, art, and other human artifacts and constructs.

We are especially likely to enact or interact with our archetypes when we are triggered, or surprised, or otherwise highly emotionally charged by another person, a relationship, an event, or a new awareness or learning ("Aha!"). In addition, we act on and react to them based on our attitude toward change, writ large or small into the fabric of our lives. As a result, life becomes a mosaic of interwoven archetypal images or patterns that may either form or inhibit behaviors, thoughts, feelings, and/or attitudes.

How many times have you wondered, "How did I do this?" or "What got into me?" or "Where did THAT come from?" Have you responded or reacted with great surprise regarding something you said, or did, or thought? If you give it some thought, you'll probably find that you've done this many times before.

I would suggest that, when we question ourselves, we may be "in the grip" of a particular archetype, or an archetypal pattern or a complex of archetypes. Often, these are unconscious, or subconscious. That's precisely why we're surprised by ourselves – we don't see and we're not aware of what we're doing and why we're doing it.

Archetypes are powerful entities in our lives, and beyond measure. They may serve as our allies and mentors, or they may serve as competitors, or challengers – or both, and anything in between.

The "Play" of Archetypes

As are our lives, archetypes themselves are not static or fixed, though we may become enamored of them or feel stuck with them. (This feeling of enthrallment and stasis happens in our lives, too.) Archetypes are dynamic and evolving forces. One or more may pass temporarily in front of us and become either a core aspect of our archetypal totem or a transitory feature of a particular circumstance, situation, or relationship that we are working through. Being a lover comes to mind here, or being a trickster.

These and other archetypal images and figures may play a key or core role in our lives at a given moment. They may also then give way to something else, or take a place in our background or back story. They will always exist, yet their place in the momentary present will inevitably shift as our circumstances do.

Let's use an example that might be familiar to you. In Latin, there is a term to denote the eternal child, one who never grows up or out of the child's place/role/archetype. It is known as either the *puer aeternus* (male) or *puella aeterna* (female). One of the best known of these in the English literary canon is Peter Pan. In fact, many psychologists refer to this behavior and its concurrent attitudes as an *archetypal complex* – or a cluster of archetypal patterns enmeshed as one.

World literature, the arts, poetry, fairy tales, and other stories that utilize the sociological process known as "transgenerational transmission" convey this archetype in all its splendor, with all its inherent challenges, adventures, and fascination. This large and cumbersome term indicates a progressive process of passing information and data down from one generation to another, though the ways that this may occur do in fact change over the generations. Witness, in fact, that for many of us in middle age, our grandparents never had the pleasure of playing or working with cell phones, computers, WiFi, cablevision, and a host of other apparati that many now consider treasured toys and mandatory work gadgets.

The puer figures, as archetypes, are both simultaneously embedded and transcendent in our human world. We all know adults who exhibit these characteristics. In fact, we may at times be frustrated at seeing this in ourselves, or being told it is so. The *puer* can fuse with or infuse aspects of our persona or our shadow at times, due to restimulation, triggering, regressive behavior, or even sentiment.

On a broader level, whether or not we know, observe, or experience the puer directly, it is still there, known if not present. As such, this archetype may transcend our own individual direct experience. In this way (as with all archetypes), it simply exists in the more abstract collective of our unconscious. It may touch down gently or strike hard at any moment due to foreseen or unforeseen circumstances.

There may be a time (or times) in each of our lives when we are reticent, or doubtful, or downright enraged about having to grow up, to be accountable, to accept full responsibility for our lives, our words, and our actions. Some might say, either seriously or sarcastically, that this is, in fact, the very definition of adolescence, asking, "Well, isn't that the process of adolescence at work?"

For some, the eternal child may be a core aspect of themselves or their personalities or personal struggles. Others may touch it at one point, or more than once, each time kissing it goodbye as they move forward toward and through adulthood. For still others, whether they are thrust into adulthood too early or in a timely manner, they embrace it with a benign sense of acceptance. For all, the puer/puella archetype is still out there, whether or not it touches, embraces, or chokes them at some point or another. This is true for the long list of archetypes and their patterns. No two lives or *archetypal totems* are fully alike.

The Archetypal Totem

Let's deconstruct the concept of an "archetypal totem" that was referenced earlier. What is a totem? A totem is a spirit being, sacred object, or symbol that serves as an emblem of a group of people, such as a family, clan, lineage, or tribe. While the term totem is Ojibwe (natives from the north of the Great Lakes area between the USA and Canada), belief in tutelary spirits and deities is not limited to indigenous peoples of the Americas. It is common to a number of cultures worldwide.

However, the traditional people of those cultures have words for their guardian spirits in their own languages. They do not call or refer to these spirits or symbols as totems. It is a generic term utilized to identify a sacred element of our human selves that comes to bear in our daily experience. Thus, an archetypal totem is a dynamic set of these spirits, as archetypes, that present themselves as one or more aspects of our personalities, our identities, our personal and interpersonal dynamics.

As we continue to explore the complexities and intricacies of archetypes, you may find yourself building your own personal, unique, current archetypal totem. Much as some Native American and Canadian "totem poles" have been created over time, yours will include those archetypes, patterns, and complexes to which you feel yourself most drawn. It will be influenced by, or focused on, a specific time period in your life.

Over the long arc of your life, the particular elements in your personal archetypal totem will morph, fade, burn in, and possibly burn out, much like a shooting star. Yet, some archetypes may remain steady, as core aspects of one's inner self. All of this is mutable within the universe of archetypes.

- In understanding your journey of examination to hone in on your archetypal totem of this (or any given) moment, focus on these critical questions:

- What images recur in your dreams, to the extent you are aware of them?

- In the arts, what characters, personalities, temperaments, and idiosyncrasies are you drawn to?

- What do you notice with regard to your closest friends, colleagues, and family member that both excites and repels you?

- In your own inner/emotional landscape, what feelings and thoughts are most prevalent, and which do you try to avoid?

Once you begin to determine some clear responses, archetypes and totems have ways of "announcing" themselves to you. First and foremost, on this journey of exploration you are bringing along with you your powers of discernment and insight, your experiences and observations of self/other/world, and perhaps the most precious journey-gift of all: the time to reflect. Once you've determined that these are along with you, you're ready to go!

Of particular note, of course, is when things along the way get fuzzy or confused and clarity is not forthcoming. This is, in itself, both remarkable and a normal part of the journey. Time not only heals most wounds, but it gives us the opportunity to deepen our focus and determination. Lack of clarity is best understood when not judged, but only noted. In other words, reflect – don't evaluate. In time, more will become clear to you, and you will appreciate the process of discernment more deeply.

NINE

~

Archetypes and Human Identity

Be yourself... everyone else is already taken...
~ Anonymous

Archetypes, Identity, and the Self

Who are you? How do you know this? What clues and cues, what evidence, understanding, and awareness help you to determine who you are? How does any or some or all of this become clear to you – and what happens when it isn't clear, or doesn't become so? Is there more than one "you"? As humans, how consistent are we with regard to our behaviors, thoughts, actions, attitudes, and iterations of beliefs, values, and ethics? Responding to this question in particular is a challenge, both in the formulation of its content and in its clear articulation.

Consistency within one's self, personality, and temperament are among the most difficult of all human experiences to maintain over time. It is in the nature of the human condition to live and grow through change, and to change throughout our lives. The evolution and development of any living organism promotes both change and consistency with regard to maintaining our life-giving and life-enhancing functions.

Archetypes are blueprints or maps for humanity and what is referred to as the "human condition." This condition is the sum total of all of our collective experiences, needs, desires, aspirations, challenges, observations, feelings, reflections, thoughts, and physical, social, emotional, recreational, intellectual, and spiritual selves rolled up into one. All of this collectively forms a global species.

Taken individually, then together, forming one coherent "self" is an amazingly – alarmingly – complex process. It's no wonder that most of us struggle with one or more aspects of our lives throughout our lifespan!

Having an archetypal awareness or approach to life may be a strong source of support and understanding as we navigate these myriad complexities, often juggling two or more at once. Applying this to ourselves and our relationships can serve as a bridge between two or more contradictions, paradoxes, or blind spots where otherwise we could not see or make a connection between people and events.

Forming an identity is a long and challenging process. One definition of identity is "the state of fact of remaining the same one or ones, under varying aspects or conditions." Thus, consistency, more than variability, is key in developing – and then maintaining – one's identity. Academics and psychologists often think that an individual has more than one singular identity, and can also identify with more than one way of being or interacting in the world. Whether we have one or more identities, they are, at least in part, a socially constructed reality.

We are each born within and into a social environment, consisting of units we call families (sibling/s and parent/s), neighborhoods, communities, and so forth. Beyond these increasingly larger and more abstract concentric circles, we also have daily if not regular contact with local organizations and institutions including but not limited to schools, clubs, gyms, playmates, after-school programs, familial relatives, and more.

All of our human interactions with others combine to form our on-going and dynamic "social realities" and who we become over time is largely based on the values, beliefs, convictions, attitudes, and perspectives that we grow to understand. If contradictory, we select what feels most ethical and moral to us as individuals. Thus, we personally construct, at least in part through choice and preference, our socially constructed reality, which we live in and with on a daily basis.

Given this personal construction of our individual reality over the course of our lives, the individuals and our relationships within it involve change as we develop over time. The archetypes that speak most boldly and loudly to us are those that we have contact with both consciously and unconsciously. Our daily interactions with others though our activities, dialogues, study, work, and recreation evoke strong emotions, both in the moment and sometimes long afterwards. The archetypes that emanate from these experiences, including characters, emotions, places, and values, play an important, if difficult to discern, role in our responses and behaviors.

Since we live and journey with these archetypes, they then become an aspect of our identity or identities. We identify with certain archetypes more than others – whether by choice, default, unconscious process (dreams, "Freudian slips," déjà vu, and other such incidents and phenomena), or general happenstance. This doesn't necessarily mean, however, that those we are primarily drawn to form our identity/ies exclusively. Here's where the archetypal formation/generation process can become quite interesting!

Here we must at least briefly revisit the shadow, a primary consideration in Jung's psychological world view. As we've seen, our shadow is that part of ourselves which we (try to) keep out of public view. As such, we either consciously or unconsciously restrain, contain, and disdain aspects of ourselves we don't want others to see. Sometimes, we're not even aware of our words or actions. Thus, we're often shocked and surprised when they leap forth.

Interestingly, sometimes the shadow aspect of ourselves becomes a part of our identity, if we cannot put a lid on it. This is to say that, at those moments, we're "in the grip" of a part of ourselves we can't hold back: feelings of intense anger, rage, and outrage, along with, perhaps, such related emotions as jealousy, and grief, to name but a few.

When we're stuck or overwhelmed by these feelings, they take hold of us, and sometimes dominate the more positive aspects of our identities. In these periods (moments, hours, days, or weeks) we're out of control – even if temporarily. Thus, there are situations and times when unwanted aspects of ourselves enter into our identity or identities. We may find ourselves in conflict internally or with others, in therapy, or in trouble. Our personal awareness – in Daniel Goleman's terms, social and emotional intelligences – is key in steering us through these dramas.

In coming to form core aspects of ourselves such as identity, we draw on a wide continuum of what's accessible to us during the early years of our growth and development. For each of us, the elements and the combinations are unique. They may be drawn from family, relatives, and friends who may serve as our mentors and role models.

The formation and development of our identity (or identities) takes place through our community, formal and non-formal education, travels, media, technology, values, religion, faith, and spirituality (or the lack thereof), our journeys and journeying, and the plethora of other endeavors in human experience. And yet, how many of us can articulate precisely what our identity is, or what our identities are? To do so requires thought, reflection, and perhaps the feedback of others. It's core, but it's intangible as well.

> It is only with the heart
> that one can see rightly;
> What is essential
> is invisible to the eye…
> ~ Antoine de Sainte-Exupéry, *The Little Prince*

Let's shift now to focus on archetypes as the primary building blocks that shape our human identity or identities. This exploration, in and of itself, is a human journey. We're exploring, turning things over and under, uncertain at moments as to direction and movement. Sometimes an aspect is uncertain, unclear, and undefined. What will you bring along with you, as we undertake this journey of exploration and self-discovery?

The Earliest Emergence of Archetypes

Because we experience archetypes directly as well as understanding them in their more general forms, we know that archetypes exist simultaneously both in the material and the intangible worlds. Many come from the natural world – the sun, the moon, stars, planets, water, fire, heat, ice, thunder, lightning, snow, wilderness, mountains, oceans, stone. Others reach us through the animal and mammal kingdoms. Still others speak to us from the humanly-constructed world: money, power, skyscrapers, guns, clocks, bridges, tunnels, eyeglasses, cars, airplanes, and the wheel, to mention but a few of thousands. Finally, there are archetypes that evolve in us through our emotional fields, such as anger, sadness, grief, ecstasy, pain, suffering, sympathy, empathy, and love. In our lives, we are mostly responsive, reactive, or initiatory with all these archetypal fields and clusters as we perceive or come into contact with them.

From their earliest post-partum moments, most newborns are highly active and engaged. They are interacting with humans, usually adults, and sometimes with a range of implements, tools, equipment, and whatever else is necessary to achieve a safe and successful birth. In those first moments, whether they know it or not, newborns are forming "fight or flight" responses, and have only the language of tears (crying), reflexes, sleeping, and perhaps babbling to communicate with their outer world. It is from this humblest of beginnings that the human lifecycle commences.

From those early moments, our personalities slowly begin to emerge. People, places, events, situations, initiatives, and responses to internal and external data serve to form our understanding of the world and our earliest experiences as a being within it. It's too complex to remember later on. For the time being, as infants, we're living in a whirling stream of consciousness: everything and everyone everywhere is new to us.

As we learn to connect with and make attachments to things, people, and places, they begin to get a foothold at the core of our lives. These early experiences have the opportunity to take on added significance – positive or negative – in our earliest years. This can mean that they are more than what they are: we are dependent upon them. We often cry at the very idea of change, loss, or abandonment (and parents often do as well!).

There is no object permanence as we begin our journey as newborns; once something or someone exits our sphere of vision, it is as though they are gone – forever. And the reaction is strong, swift, and immediate – tears, tantrums, flailing, wailing – the whole nine yards. Attachment and connection are primary concerns as we inch our way, over many years, toward independence and autonomy.

What we're looking at here is also the emergence of archetypes in our lives as they first appear. Like heated molecules in a contained space, we as newborns and infants are "switched on": we're vaguely aware, at first, of the people, faces, foods, drinks, objects, and sounds that surround us. All come and go, touching us, infiltrating us, entering our space whether we ask for, want, or need them. The pace is exhausting: everything is new, and so we sleep and nap and rest at length, giving our young selves the needed rest and recovery time to gear up once again for more novelty, and possibly, adversity.

Soon enough, these archetypal experiences become some part of us. They tame us, and we begin to anticipate them – the beginning of regularity, of continuity, of relationship. Not all of us are fortunate or blessed to anticipate goodness and positivity during this critical period. Things go wrong all the time. If this is the case, we revert back to our more primitive and limited states of expressing negative emotion. And so it becomes entirely possible that we get caught up in a negative archetype.

This negativity needn't be a lifelong event, and often is not. As our life circumstances and challenges change, so, too, can the way we read and interact with archetypes. This means we can transition from seeing and reacting to a negative archetype and move on to its positive form – or vice versa.

If the negative version of an archetype remains with us for any consistent period of time during our sensitive earliest developmental stages, it may well factor into our early identity development. Fear, insecurity, shyness, passivity, or their opposites are all compensatory strategies to deal with our early childhood hurts. Unless they are specifically addressed through some sort of targeted intervention, as youngsters we may identify with these states of being, and they find their ways into our personal identities. For example, the bully or the braggart often overcompensates by acting out in public to mask an inner feeling of insecurity.

Along the continuum of human experience, in our earliest forms of being, we may (hopefully, but not predictably) also come into contact with positives – exemplars, s/heroes, or role models. Later in early life, we'll come to call them mentors, coaches, and teachers. Our path to self-reliance, independence, interdependence, and accountability usually brings one or more stable adults along the way.

Sometimes our earliest connections with the adults or peers in our lives are loving, benevolent, patient, and caring. At the least, we are left with some of those impressions, part of our waking time, and we want more. Or, we may come to expect and anticipate more. If more is given, we are satiated. If not, we're hurt and disappointed. Healthy and positive archetypes and behaviors emerge from good early care and relationships. These leave an indelible and potentially lasting image with us, and we grow from them.

Recall here, again, the characters and characterizations in L. Frank Baum's *The Wizard of Oz* books and the movies made from them.

These are some of the deepest, longest-lasting archetypal evocations in the canon of modern American literature and film. The two witches, in particular, come to mind: the Wicked Witch of the West, and the Good Witch of the East. They're both witches, whatever that means! But: they are also quintessential opposites of one another, and our experience of them through Dorothy indicates her hope, her confusion, and her pathos. These archetypes will be within her for a long time to come, whether we see them or not, and whether she becomes consciously aware of them, or not.

Each of us carries these blueprints within us, each archetype in all its iterations from positive and supportive to negative and detrimental. Our birth-through-death experiences bring some aspects of each along this continuum to fruition and our lived reality.

Archetypes and Identity: Which Defines the Other?

This is the by-now infamous, age-old question, slightly revised: which comes (or came) first – the chicken or the egg? As always, the response is a matter of perspective. While the very concept and term "archetype" is not even a century old yet – Jung coined it in 1919 – the idea has been around as long as humankind has walked the earth.

As Jung has written, archetypes are embedded in our *collective unconscious*, meaning they have been "hard-wired" into the core of each human being's very being and existence. Why else would the vast majority of human beings worldwide have a fear of snakes? We are born with this; it is a core part of our nature and condition.

Jung himself wrote and lectured that archetypes, both in form and in concept, are universal. He placed the construct of archetypes within the collective unconscious. For him, and for others in the generations following his groundbreaking work, the vast majority and huge number of archetypes are elemental to all cultures and beings across history and place. If, as Jung postured, archetypes arise out of this universal unconsciousness, then their actual embodiment or manifestation comes forth in each human being on a more personal level based on their actual lived experience with any and all archetypes.

Those archetypes that become activated within each one of us first enter our personal unconscious. We are initially unconscious of them, yet our lived experiences may bring them into our personal consciousness. This is because we come to understand how our unconscious may then trigger a behavior, thought, feeling, or utterance that we may discover "came out of nowhere," and this nowhere is "now here": it comes from our hidden place and surprised us to now recognize our response as real, no longer hidden, frozen, or unconscious.

Archetypes permeate all aspects of our being. From the creation of ego and self-esteem to functional and dysfunctional relationships to our drive to work and make good in the world, they serve to add dimension and depth to our considerations of growth, development, aging, and death.

In times of trouble and transition, archetypes may serve as anchors that can ground us in a larger reality than our pain and suffering. In good times, they help us to better understand and construct and steer our positivity forward. Whether we are clear and conscious of them or not, archetypes are alive, dynamic, and evolving within us; they may erupt, disrupt, interrupt, even corrupt us, if we cannot bring some aspect(s) of them into our daily and conscious reality.

As described earlier, Adolf Hitler is a particularly heinous example. He was, as has been documented many times and in many places, unconscious of his anger at his rejection by art schools run by Jews. His personal unconscious thus produced a negative archetype.

Given his negative experience in this regard, he created a stereotype of Jews as evil, pernicious people individually and as a collective culture/religion. Left unchecked, unexplored, and untethered, his negative projections onto this cohort ran rampant when he came into power a couple of decades after these rejection events in the late 1890s.

In a most gruesome and egregious way, his negative stereotypes (and his archetypes) exploded, with tragic results. Ask yourself, what might have happened – or not happened – had Hitler entered into therapy, or a loving relationship, or a deeper awareness of himself and his frustration after receiving three consecutive rejection letters? How might history and the world have changed, and changed for the betterment of all?

It may well be that there are more examples of human goodness and positively-charged archetypes at work in the world than their converse. However, this doesn't mitigate the damage that Hitler and others like him have perpetrated. Modern-day heroes and heroines – all peacemakers on the international stage – have engaged themselves with warm and loving archetypes. A brief but not exhaustive list might hold such luminaries as Mahatma Gandhi, Mother Teresa, Martin Luther King, Rosa Parks, Nelson Mandela, Eleanor Roosevelt, Bishop Desmond Tutu, Malala Yousafzai, and Pope Francis. Whom would you add to this list?

These positive archetypes have no doubt helped inspire and focus their work: angel, guiding spirit, mentor, teacher, guide, Good Father/Good Mother, and so forth. We collectively look to their good work and graceful manner of being when our world feels troubled, as it is now. We draw lessons and parallels, support, and inspiration from them to propel us forward into greater harmony within ourselves and with one another.

The Reality (or Illusion) of Choice

How do we select our individual archetypes and create our archetypal totems? Or do they find us? Since inspiration is often what propels leaders to take risks and champion causes no matter how unpopular, many believe that they are characterized by archetypes that offer inspiration. For instance, the Rev. Dr. Martin Luther King, Jr. often spoke of heading to the mountaintop, a metaphor, perhaps, for seeking to gain inspiration and insight from a higher power.

The question of free choice, the autonomy to select our archetypes, is worthy of further scrutiny. We all grow up with particular socially-constructed concepts and practices, but we can each make the choice to opt out of them. If we don't do so on a conscious level, it may be that the default is, instead, to allow cultural norms to simply carry us.

It takes courage, patience, and deep conviction to stand up to power, especially the type of power that is seen and known as "power over" oneself or others. As we've seen time and again, people who do so put their lives and the lives of their family at risk. This is of universal significance.

Archetypes that give our lives greater meaning are sometimes the tools that help us to carry forth our missions and visions. Archetypes of hope, forgiveness, love, intimacy, strength, and resilience are examples. We have to want – or even need – the strength and gravitas of archetypes to have the boldness and conviction to move ahead.

If we have the strength and passion of these beliefs, then we can make a free choice to accept, and even welcome, archetypes and their images and patterns into our lives and our work. If we do not, then benign acceptance of those archetypes that maintain the sociocultural status quo (or denial of their existence) remain within us.

The formation of a human identity is not a simple, straight-forward evolution. There are both internal and external complexities involved. Since human beings are not perfect beings, there are also contradictions, paradoxes, and inconsistencies.

Our lives – along with our personalities, temperaments, moods, and preferences – are a mix of personal choice and selection, as well as things coming down from above, or at least, from elsewhere. This is not to say it is fatalistic and predetermined, although many religions and faith-based practices do feature this viewpoint and value.

Either way, the roles of culture and one's heritage and ancestry loom large indeed. Identity formation is a delicate and dynamic balance of nature and nurture and their ongoing interplay.

In the end, as we come to further understand the roles of identity and archetype, we begin to sense and experience how deeply interconnected both are. Many people build their identities by choice, given the cultural "allowance" to do so. Part of their process is to relate (even if unconsciously) to particular archetypes and their patterns.

In addition, there are times when specific archetypes are affixed, placed, even forced onto and into us. We may do something unconsciously, and suddenly we're branded a "bad guy" or a "good girl," or something else, even if that was not our intention or interest. There is no formula, no equation, by which all humans integrate the archetypes and the identity. That process is one of constant folding and unfolding, discovery, and recovery. It is an evolution that draws on mind, psyche, spirit, soul, intellect, and body throughout the human lifespan.

Finally, who we are and how archetypes factor into our lives is also based in part on the questions we ask of ourselves and of others. Think about some of the earliest questions you might have explored in childhood: What do I want to be (or do) when I grow up? Do I ever want to get married? To have children and a family? Do I want to go to college? Beyond? What are my favorite activities? Subjects in school? What questions do you recall asking yourself and others about your world and your future as a youngster?

Our responses to these questions, as well as whom we draw upon for support as we explore them, has much to do with identity development and the calling on particular archetypes. For example, as an elementary school student growing up in the heart of New York City in the early 1960s, I became fascinated with travel, with the uniqueness of different cultures I experienced there, read about in books and *National Geographic* magazine, or saw in movies and on TV.

From an archetypal perspective, I was drawing on the archetypes of journeyer, adventurer, aspirant, and dreamer, among others. I wanted to be a *National Geographic* photographer when I was a child, not an athlete, entertainer, scientist, or even the teacher I eventually became.

I won't say that these archetypes penetrated my consciousness at an early age. Rather, I was drawn to things, people, stories, relationships, and experiences that emanated from these specific archetypes. I embraced what they meant, what they said, and how they "went about their business" in reality and in fiction.

In 1967, I took my first international trip, with my family, to the International Expo in Montreal, Canada. I saw the world there – and was I ever in bliss, with my new Kodacolor camera, documenting every moment and inch of that journey! The moon landing during the summer of 1969 was also a signature event for me. It was a cause for celebration, and for great curiosity and exploration. Stepping-off points such as these have had a profound impact on me throughout my life, and I suspect always will.

By now, a great deal of this archetypal complex has been thoroughly and creatively integrated into my life and my world. I'd say that travel and external journeying – both as my lived experience and as my accompanying archetypes, are now core elements of my identity. The "archetypal cluster" I carry with me here includes such archetypes as the wanderer, journeyer, adventurer, pioneer, dreamer, and visionary.

My friends and colleagues know that my yearning for travel adventure calls on me to bounce out of my comfort zones every few months or I feel I will go stir-crazy. So they encourage me to head out, to be myself in this way. This allows me the space and time to seek pathways in the outer world through which I can find greater awareness and understanding by testing and challenging myself in uncomfortable (or at least unknown) situations.

Before moving on, pause for a moment to consider the current key questions that occupy you. Where do they lead you? What draws you to these questions? What information do you try to access to formulate your response or responses?

If you continue your discernment, you may likely find that you're reflecting on an archetypal level, beyond mere details and logistics, beyond even three-dimensional data. Some have said that, if there is a fourth dimension, it is time. There's an effective argument to be made that a fourth dimension may be the archetypal dimension, a comprehensive way of "complexifying" – and deepening our understanding – of ourselves, of life, of the world.

As we close this chapter, it might be helpful to conclude by reinforcing two key concepts that were its focus. First, archetypes are both universal and personalized to our unique lives, so they serve to emphasize the earlier notion that we move along a continuum from unique to universal. Second, this dimension is once again an example of paradox, reinforcing Jung's idea of one *and* the other rather than one or the other. In addition, this fourth dimension deepens our understanding by both simplifying and "complexifying" our perceptions of the world.

~

TEN

The Evolution and Revolution of Archetypes

*Every advance, every conceptual achievement of mankind,
has been connected with an advance in self-awareness.*

~ C. G. Jung

Time, Change, and the Human Condition

Our lives are not only evolutionary, they are revolutionary as well. For those not steeped in politics, this may seem to be a radical thought. What does a revolution have to do with the human lifespan? Why bother to link the two? In this chapter, we'll undertake a journey toward understanding what makes each life revolutionary. We'll consider how archetypes factor into and throughout our human evolution and revolution. Let's take each in turn, starting with the evolution of archetypes.

We've already touched on this in previous chapters. We've come to see that archetypes, their patterns, complexes, and totems are with us at birth, and throughout our lives. They grow in us as we develop and mature. Their dynamics and interplay influence our lives in both predictable and unknowable ways. We are in relationship with some more than others; our personal cast of archetypes changes as we do. This is personal evolution at work.

Over time, we have the opportunity to come to know ourselves with greater intimacy and awareness. We develop the clarity and consciousness to comprehend how we are driven and drawn to certain archetypes and not to others. Issues such as free choice, autonomy, and independent selection mix and mingle with concurrent experiences such as our culture and its elements, the balance and integration of the nature/nurture binary, and the trajectory of human history through time and space.

The human condition has remained true to its essence while also changing in obvious and subtle ways over the long arc of time. We are still inherently social beings, interdependent to a lesser or greater extent on one another. We have always set up collectivist units – families or clans or tribes. From these social units, we continue to expand into communities or neighborhoods. From there, it is onward and outward to progressively larger, more complex, and increasingly abstract circles of connection and belonging.

Historically, we have evolved from hunter-gatherers to a largely post-industrial, even post-technological age. Over time, our lives have changed significantly – but not our basic needs, instincts, drives, and many of our desires and aspirations. We generally live longer, yet, still, we die.

Plus ça change, plus c'est la même chose.
(The more things change, the more they remain the same.)

Although written by the French journalist Jean-Baptiste Alphonse Karr in 1849, I first came across this expression in John Knowles' 1959 novel, *A Separate Peace.* It seems particularly poignant and pertinent here.

How do things – and how does life itself – evolve? Is there an impetus toward stasis and the status quo, or is there always the inevitable push for change and growth and development? And to what extent are these separate and distinct from one another? With these questions, we are once again looking into the vortex of the age-old nature/nurture debate.

We can cut to the chase here by once again invoking Jung's idea that it's not a question of one *or* the other, but rather one *and* the other. There is no light without darkness, no day without night, no hot without cold, no joy without sadness. While it moves ever forward, evolution is essentially a stop-and-go process.

What we've come to understand from the realm of developmental psychology and developmental psychologists is just this: there are two paired phases in any developmental trajectory. There is a growth stage followed by what is known as a *moratorium*. A visual graph of this development would look like a staircase.

The growth stage enables us to try out and explore novelty, to take risk and stretch ourselves beyond our comfort zones. During each growth period, we see and we do things differently than we have, and we screw up, make mistakes, and behave erratically and inconsistently. We're simply trying things out, seeing what works, and experimenting with our bodies and minds in novel ways to establish and attain greater competence and confidence.

Over time, this stretch period begins to recede, and there follows a moratorium, wherein we develop some degree of mastery, knowledge, coordination, and understanding, and practice it with ever more skill and efficiency. Moratoriums are hardly resting phases: our success, growth, and futures depend on the degree of mastery and consistency we can attain before pushing forward again toward greater abstraction and complexity.

In the United States, our school system is largely based on this premise. There is something called "The Plus-One Paradigm," which states that the best teaching and instruction happens precisely one small but noticeable level above what we are presently capable of, making the next step toward greater mastery achievable with time, practice, and effort.

As we work with this Plus-One Paradigm, at some point, there is a push from within us to grow, to achieve or be or do at another level, in another way. And again, we fumble, and stumble, and then make an effort to "get there" – to excel through practice. This occurs all the way through our lives. Growth and maintenance, change and steadiness, novelty to predictability. Psychologists refer to all of this as the principle of successive approximation. This is evolution in practice, at play, and at work. This is "the journey."

A Few Key Archetypes

Archetypally, the same pattern of evolution holds true. Over time, each of us generates an indelible personal imprint on our world based on all the possibilities and potential of the huge inventory of archetypes derived from our collective human experience, observation, vision, hopes, dreams, aspirations, fears, failures, and challenges.

As we develop our unique identity, we both are connected to and follow universal, then cultural, then increasingly more personalized archetypes. Because archetypes as we first meet them are actually unconscious, we are not aware of their presence, meaning, significance, and value. It is only as we learn about them, and from them, that we begin to recognize that there is something more to our lives beyond the merely tangible that offers depth and dimension to our understanding and awareness of self.

Once we begin to learn why we've done or not done something in particular, we have the potential to gain insight into that "thing" and to our own awareness of our inner self, perhaps our shadow, usually hidden from our view and the viewing of others. Our sphere here both expands and diminishes in accordance with our growth curves and the nature/nurture duality that is always present. Let's take a few examples here to bring theory and reality together.

The trickster. We all know kids – maybe we were one, once upon a time – who are "playful little devils": fun, charismatic, energetic, and at the same time, full of mischief. They excel at creatively setting up challenging situations for others to negotiate, playing games and tricks more for the fun of it all than out of maliciousness.

This is the personality, the archetype, of the trickster. They love to play, are wholly present in the moment, and are relatively unconcerned with any particular outcome. It is an aspect of another archetype that we discussed earlier, the puer or puella aeternus. But, unlike the puer, the trickster as an archetype is not limited to the domain of childhood.

Many young tricksters morph or mature into more serious and more grounded beings as adults. Yet it's also true that many who engaged the archetype and behaviors of a trickster in their youth will continue to play this out into and throughout adulthood. If so, they are apt to become increasingly sophisticated with their tricks – perhaps a lifelong obsession or idiosyncrasy.

Thus, the developmental arc or trajectory of the trickster archetype can be short or long or anything in between. It may peak in childhood, or it may not show itself until after we've had one or more mid-life crises. There is no formula here: tricksters may play out in many styles over the course of their lifetimes.

Who do you know – or relate to – who serves the trickster archetype? Certainly, they're out and about. They're entertainers and performers, athletes and everyday people. And, even if unintentionally, some are politicians. They tend to stand out in a crowd simply because they are not afraid of their own shadow and don't mind looking silly or foolish.

Groucho Marx, Charlie Chaplin's *Little Tramp*, and the mythical Kokopelli come to mind. Some well-known comedians of note with regard to this archetype would be Billy Crystal, the Borat character (played by actor Sacha Baron Cohen), Gilligan from the 1970s TV show, *Gilligan's Island*, Lucille Ball, Don Rickles, and Jim Carrey. Baseball catcher Yogi Berra, basketball player Charles Barkley, baseball pitcher Bill "Spaceman" Lee, and the entire Harlem Globetrotters basketball team come to mind as athletic tricksters.

The fool. (Also known as the simpleton/simple one, the clown, the jester, the impish one, the jokester). There are two kinds of fools:

ones who really don't know any better and are relatively clueless, and those who are exceptionally intelligent and gifted, and play the fool for fun, out of cleverness and a love of drama and histrionics. Initially, it may be hard to determine the distinction between these two. Both forms love to watch the reactions of others to their tomfoolery and sleight of hand. But it all becomes clear as we get to see and experience someone beneath the surface, and observe or interact with them in a multiplicity of varied situations.

How does the fool show up? They can make the most obvious and reasonable details in life so ridiculously complex, or confusing, that we question them or ourselves and our basic prior understanding of a given situation or circumstance. They're redundant in a hundred different ways. Frustration and eye-rolling often ensue as we witness this archetype at work. They may pretend to be (or to play) dumb or uncomprehending, slow or silly, and manifest behaviors that demonstrate these qualities. This is a specialty – and they delight in it!

But, be forewarned: there is often nothing simple about the fool. They are often complicated and complex beings, shrewd, clever, calculating, self-aware and in control of their actions, behaviors, and wordsmithing. People who play the fool engage with the archetype willingly and consciously.

Indeed, fools seem to enjoy, and even cherish, their coveted role and its archetype. It is highly social and seeks to be seen by others. Do you know anyone who's invested themselves in this behavior and its accompanying archetype? Everyone seems to know one, and the reaction is nearly always universal – they can drive us crazy, or at least to distraction. But underneath that, they are (or can be) fun!

Many fools may also be associated with trickster qualities. Sometimes, it's difficult to see a difference until one really gets to know both qualities and individuals deeply. For example, Lucille Ball, in her "I Love Lucy" shows, played both, cunningly and adroitly. Similarly, within that same TV generation, Tommy Smothers played both fool and trickster to his brother, Dickie. Don Adams, playing Maxwell

Smart in the 1960s and 1970s sitcom "Get Smart," held more of the fool archetype than that of the trickster.

Who plays the fool archetype in your world? How are they different from the tricksters mentioned above? And, how do you connect with or relate to the fool? Do you have any of the fool in you – and, if so, who or what brings it out in you, and when, where, and why? Remember, these are not always merely the outward manifestations of others – some are within us, able to be self-contained and regulated, and some appear either consciously or unconsciously.

The Lover. We ascribe several behavioral characteristics to the lover. These include, especially, passion, compassion, romance, deep connection and intimacy, and grace. Lovers are beguiling, enticing, smooth, compelling characters who draw us in by their charm, their looks, their charisma, and, at least superficially, their beneficence.

We see in the lover something – or many things – that attract us and have us yearning or dreaming to be with them. Lovers can bring us out of and beyond ourselves as we reach out to them, and commit ourselves to their care, protection, and intimacy. Hollywood, Bollywood, and Broadway are full of such characters. They are the stuff of library shelves, world poetry, screenplay and script, and posters on teenagers' bedroom walls. We adore them, though they may not know or even notice us.

The challenge with the lover archetype is that it remains one way only, more or less. We seek, we want, and we have an overpowering desire for them. We idolize at least some of their qualities, even idealize them as over and above us. We are overtaken and smitten by their beauty, handsomeness, grace, elegance, sexiness, "bad boy/bad girl" naughtiness, even their wholesomeness. However we characterize them, they are people who evoke great passion, even lust, within us in our "everyday ordinariness." As such, there is a distance between them and us, as well as a power asymmetry. We can really never have them in the sense that we think we want them.

Lovers are really not available to us on the carnal *and* tangible level that we may seek or dream about. Because of this, there is often even greater yearning, and we are often overwhelmed, even paralyzed, lest we get too close. Remember, we are speaking of the archetype of the lover here, not someone who is genuinely beloved.

One lover – with the greatest love of words – was the 13th century Persian Sunni Muslim poet, Jalal ad-Din Muhammad Balkhi Mawlawi – best known to most of us as Rumi. His poems have been widely translated around the world into dozens of languages, and many speak to the power of love, in unconditional, unrequited, intimate, yearning, and passionate language.

The Warrior. We shouldn't mistake or confuse warriors for soldiers. Soldiers fight in combat, often violently and with the intent of harming, maiming, or killing "the enemy"; warriors take up a cause and will pursue their side of a given conflict beyond the mere use of violence.

The archetype of the warrior engages in a repertoire of nonviolent tactics and strategies, such as strikes, picketing, petitions, compelling oration, political or economic methods, and the arts (as in "guerilla theatre"). Their "combat" may well be psychological, social, emotional, even recreational – without the stated intent of harming another in any personal manner. The means and the ends, as practiced by soldiers and warriors, couldn't be more different. Yet the two are all too often conflated.

Although the word "war" forms the first half of the larger term, the war itself is one that is often waged with words or other forms of human behavior and thought that seek to make a point without injuring another person. The archetype of the warrior is one of activism, engagement, of the person who does not settle for a compromise or back down. Warriors step up for the betterment of all, especially those in subordinate positions in the world's pecking order. The "Warrior for Peace" or "The War on Poverty" are two such examples.

Other examples are the gentle warriors who, with their passionate and compassionate convictions, have waged war against some of the many ills and diseases within our world, and their own societies and cultures. Individuals such as Mahatma Gandhi, The Reverend Dr. Martin Luther King Jr., Nelson Mandela, Rosa Parks, Eleanor Roosevelt, Benazir Bhutto, Helen Keller, Alice Paul, Harriet Tubman, and Marie Curie are among the many who exemplify this archetype.

The Mystic. The archetype of the mystic is the dreamer, a visionary, achronistic (beyond time), and engaged in the past or future. The mystic invokes mystery, myth, and mysticism. In doing so, the mystic calls in aspects that may not be tangible to a more world-based and grounded individual. Mystics are seekers, looking beyond what is most immediately and expediently present and available. In doing so, they often call out a warning or an invitation to others to follow their lead, and to consider their words and images.

Mystics live beyond the world of the material. They transcend what they may consider the trivial pursuits of the common person. They may do so by concerning themselves with the unseen, the abstract, or even what is considered nonsense. Mystics envisage the future, engage with beings and narratives not yet seen or told, and hold out either hope or nihilism, based on what calls to them. There is often holiness associated with them, their behaviors, and their statements.

In many cultures, mystics are demonized or negated. Few are taken seriously by the population at large. If they develop a following, it is often trivialized or marginalized as "fringe" and otherwise largely discounted. Often, the lack of understanding serves to disconnect the bridge between past, present, and future, or between the material world and one less concrete.

When considered seriously, however, mystics may serve as bridges between here and there or now and then, the connector of opposites that those more dually-inclined cannot imagine or hold. Mystics have been considerable forces of strength, knowledge, and wisdom when listened to, when given space to share their beliefs and understandings with the world-at-large. The early 20th century Russian mystic, Grigori Rasputin, seems to fit this bill very clearly.

Given this definition and terminology, other known mystics may or may not be familiar to you. For example, Pythagoras is known to history as a genius-level mathematician born in 570 BCE. However, he is better known by classical scholars as a mystic who was centuries ahead of his time due to his unique doctrine that the soul does not die but returns as many times as necessary to be pure and ready to move on to the next realm. Dogen, a Japanese-born Buddhist monk of the mid-13th century, emphasized the unheard of integration of the study of the intellect with meditative practices as a pathway toward self-enlightenment. Finally, Rumi (Jalalad-Din Muhammad Rumi), born in 13th-century Persia – now part of Afghanistan – was not only one of the greatest poets of the Arabic world, but also a mystic who embraced and extolled the concept of a loving reunion with a loving God.

The Earth (or Great) Mother. The Earth Mother is a universal symbol and archetype of fertility, of the giving of endless spiritual and emotional support and wordly wisdom, guidance, and love. She is empathic; she sustains life and being in and of the living by fostering growth, development, transformation, and connection to other sentient beings. She is sought after both consciously and unconsciously, in dreams, poetry, music, and dance. In the US and elsewhere, we hold special rituals, celebrations, and days in her honor: Earth Day, May Day, Mother's Day, among others.

At the same time, there is a shadow side, less known, regarding the Earth or Great Mother: she may be seen as controlling, manipulative at times, and temperamental if not pleased. As only the earth can, she can poison and kill ("magic" mushrooms are sometimes not the healing type!), and can offer weather events that wipe out entire populations (the 40-day flood of Noah's Ark, as well as current disasters due to flood, fire, tornado, hurricane, earthquake, and tsunami, to mention a few). This is further proof of the duality and unification of opposites that Jung frequently spoke of.

The Virgin Mary is seen by many in the Christian faith tradition as being exemplary of the archetype of the Great Mother, or Earth Mother. In Hinduism, Devi Adi Parashakti, the Mother Goddess, assumes this role, nurturing and sustaining all under her care. In human terms, we might extend this archetype to the benevolent Good Witch of the East in *The Wizard of Oz*. Some might associate this Mother archetype with the "Early or Pioneering Mother" of one's nation or country, such as Golda Meir in Israel, Justice Nasira Iqbal in Pakistan, or Aung San Suu Kyi in Myanmar. As goddesses, there were qualities of inhuman perfection among them. In real-life human terms, perfection is not possible, and yet those named here have been associated with the qualities and qualifications inherent in this particular archetype, despite their human flaws and failures.

The Wise Old Man. Also known as *senex* (Latin for "Old Man"), the sage, or *sophos*, the wise old man is the center of many tales worldwide over time. Archetypally speaking, the Wise Old Man is gentle, generous, understanding, patient, kind, tolerant, benevolent, and thoughtful. He offers his wisdom with clarity and love, and cares greatly for those whose lives he touches. He is generally learned in the ways of the world, has great depth in his soul, and moves, thinks, and speaks with great respect and consideration for all others. The Wise Old Man carries the qualities of magnanimity and equanimity at all times. He lives in a state of grace and ease, and his efforts help to ease the worldy burdens of those around him who seek him out. He mentors others to help "ground them" and support their forward movement in life.

Of course, as with all archetypes, there is a downside to The Wise Old Man, which manifests in particular ways. At times, he can seem absent-minded, incoherent, and foolish. With all of his wisdom and the power of such strength as an asset, he can be petulant, and may misuse his power as a control tactic. An interesting note to consider here is that the antithetical or opposing archetype to that of The Wise Old Man is that of the *puer aeternus* (*Peter Pan* et al.).

Examples of The Wise Old Man in history, literature, and mythology include Merlin from the *Legends of King Arthur* in Great Britain, Nestor from Homer's *The Iliad*, Tiresias from Homer's *The Odyssey*, *Oedipus Rex*, Zarathustra (the Persian sage), the Seven Sages of Greece, the Seven Sages of the Bamboo Grove (China), and Sages of Talmudic Law (Judaism) including Yohanan ben Zakkai, Hillel I, and Shammai.

The cataloguing of archetypes is indeed unending, revealing so much about our universe, our planet, our world, its cultures, religions, communities, and the human family. There is a huge and captivating collection of books, other writings, and art in all its forms dedicated to the articulation and embodiment of these archetypes for all humanity to consider. I urge the interested reader to sample these resources. We are all the wiser and the richer for doing so.

Before moving on, let's pause for a moment. Perhaps the descriptions above have brought out some emotion – affection or otherwise – and transported you to a different place or time. Maybe they've connected you to different thoughts, people, images, or reflections of past or dreamt-of experiences.

If you've not done so already, this may be a good moment to contemplate opportunities you have had in your life with people (real or imagined) who bring out some of these qualities and characteristics, and then consider how you may have responded to them. This may give you some greater insight as to how – and to what extent – you may be fueled by any one or more of these archetypal depictions. Please, pause to consider!

The "Commons" of Archetypes

The examples of archetypes in action described in the previous section have several common characteristics:

- Most of us know one or more individuals who manifest these elements, and therefore these archetypes.

- There's almost always a dark/heavy side and a bright/light side to each of them.

- Their behaviors and behavioral patterns crystallize as their humans envelop and engage with them, so both the humans and their archetypes are seen ever more clearly.

- There may be fusion – and/or confusion – between the person and their archetype/s and their behaviors and patterns. Clarity and vagueness may go in and out of presence.

Do you see any other commonalities among these and other archetypes as they manifest in their human form? It can be fascinating to discern patterns among them. If you have either experienced or witnessed the influence of archetypes, then perhaps you are seeking an ever-deepening understanding and awareness of their meaning and impact, both small and large.

From Human Evolution to Human Revolution

Let's journey now from *evolution* to *revolution*. This is not the seismic shift you might be thinking it is. Let's shorten each word to deconstruct this idea. What "evolves" also "revolves." Both are highly dynamic words and concepts. They indicate action and activity, either within one's self or between two or more objects or beings. Sun and earth. Earth and moon. Each evolves within itself, over time. In addition, each revolves around the other.

We are probably more familiar with the political meaning of revolution than the evolutionary nature of this word. On the one hand, revolution can be taken to mean or involve a fundamental change in political structure and organization through the overthrow or renunciation of one government or ruler and the substitution of another by the governed.

Beyond this, revolution can also mean a sudden, radical, or complete change in anyone, any way of thinking, being, or doing, or a basic or entire changeover in any system, organization, or institution. From a change perspective, or an evolutionary approach, revolutions are more normal over time than we might expect.

Revolution is at once as simple and complex as a snake shedding its skin, or a chrysalis metamorphizing into a butterfly. These are everyday occurrences across a species of beings. They are natural, anticipated, and expected. They are also quite profound, manifesting both total vulnerability and the utmost resiliency at the same time.

We worry, in fact, if they do not happen within a carefully observed and normative time frame. Why, if we humans accept that such occurrences take place with such regularity within other species, should we be so reactive to revolutions as they transpire within our own? Are we scared of change, as inevitable as it is in every aspect of our existence? And, if so, might this fear be at least in part based on our foreknowledge of death?

On the micro level, revolution is a personal or collective transition that can transform our world, or perhaps our understanding or perception of it, and, therefore, of ourselves. If a way we do things grows old, stale, and outmoded, and is no longer working for us – and we're aware of it – then we have essentially two choices: (1) do nothing, and remain stuck and trapped by it, or (2) find a way to change and allow new pathways for action and attitude. We've surely all been on both sides of this coin. Not surprisingly, archetypes have the same two sides: one opting for maintenance of the status quo, and the other hoping for, holding out for, and trying to make changes.

Revolution is about change and transition. It's also about a journey from the old to the new, from known to unknown, from past and present to present and future. All transitions, rites of passage, rituals, and life markers involve these elements, although not all are revolutionary.

If our attitudes shift in a fundamental way, then we are more likely to go through a transformation or revolution – change with a capital "C." Since attitudes are more pervasive than behaviors, major shifts here are likely to be more significant than the change in a specific and delimited behavior.

However, there are behaviors and actions that are revolutionary: giving up an addiction, a change in one's status (married to divorced, single to married, a new degree, job, career, or moving to a different place, among others). Think on this for a moment: what, if any, revolutionary changes have you made for yourself over the course of your lifetime?

As our attitudes, behaviors, even our values and ethics change over the course of a lifetime, so do our relationships to the archetypes in general and our archetypes in particular. Rare indeed is the person born with the same set of relationships with their birth archetypes as the ones they leave the world with. Over time, these changes may be small and subtle, or anywhere else on the small-to-large or subtle-to-flagrant continuum.

An Abbreviated Case Study

A decade or so ago, it was revolutionary (small "r") for me to acknowledge a change as I approached a particular birthday in early mid-life, I had actually crossed over on the Myers-Briggs Type Indicator from extraverted (E) to introverted (I). I began to see myself, my relationships, my work, and my world from an entirely new perspective. This was transformational for me: revolutionary, in fact. The "E" to "I" shift permeated so many aspects of my being, *me*, that, for a little while I was stunned to see and say and act upon things that were so radically different.

Gone, in some measure, was what I had long considered my normal and typical way of doing things. For examples, I began to appreciate and hold more intimate gatherings and get-togethers at my home rather than large ones; I learned to love keeping my own company more; I took on more solitary activities and avocations such as reading, gardening, and photography, rather than team sports and committees.

Similarly, just a few years ago I came to realize that I no longer had the same early-to-midlife passion for full-time employment. I found that working as a higher education administrator for 60 to 70 hours weekly no longer was mandatory on my always-evolving bucket list.

The very notion that I could choose not to continue with this life/ workstyle, and could, instead, think more openly and freely about other ways to earn a living was in and of itself radical, another small "r" revolution of sorts. It defined the way I would spend my days and my energies. It also added a new dimension to my identity, my lifestyle, and my vision and mission for the next chapter of my life.

At the very least, I needed a time out, the kind of sabbatical that life usually doesn't offer, although I was privileged as a lifelong academic to work in institutions that offered faculty half-year and full-year "time outs" to pursue other passions in their professional calling. I had previously taken two of these, and learned that I love having greater control over my time and greater spontaneity as well. I needed and wanted this, badly.

In my most recent professional capacity, I had virtually blown myself up, overextended myself mentally, emotionally, and physically, and given up most of what I loved in my community and social and intellectual circles. It was high time to rest, relax, reflect – and write! The images I was having and dreaming about were far, far away from classrooms, chairing meetings, facilitating committees, working with trustees, leading senior staff gatherings and retreats, and the like. I took a long time out, my own personal sabbatical, forgoing some benefits, such as salary and health insurance, but gaining others far beyond what academia offered (no pre-approved plan, not owing work to any entity after its conclusion, no pre-ordained start and end dates).

In time, my energies to opt back into "the game" – as a newly-re-committed and rebalanced elder in a senior academic administrator role – returned to me, and I decided to take it on again one final time, giving to myself, my colleagues, and my institution all that I had culled through experience and knowledge and practice over the four previous decades. A new and broader me re-emerged, dedicated to equanimity and better balance between work and life. My motto for these last few years in the full-time workforce became "I am working to live, rather than living to work."

In both examples, my archetypal composition shifted. No longer was I holding on to all the archetypes that had carried me to this point, nor was I in their grip. As I made changes within and without, so too, did my archetypal spectrum change: out with some of the old, in with some of the new.

Specifically, I moved from a trickster to a mentor; from a mover and shaker toward a contemplative; and from a warrior to a peacemaker. These were significant changes in my identity, priorities, time allocation, and understanding of self. They added up to structural as well as daily operational changes, in that I began to view myself from a different set of lenses. As I changed in these ways, so, too, did my perception of the world, the people around me, and my living/working/social relationships with them.

Recap

Both words, evolution and revolution, hold many of the same connotations: dynamic, transitional/transitory, internal and external, change(s) in perception and understanding of "reality," past/present/future orientations, and experientially-based. And, as we've already seen, archetypes hold many similar aspects as these two concepts.

I would argue that, in fact, life is about all of these things. Life is about how we learn to adapt to continuously changing circumstances and situations. In a previous chapter, we discussed the two absolute givens in life, birth and death, and proposed a third: the journey between the two. All journeying invites and instigates change; in that respect, our givens should perhaps be birth, death, and change. Within the frames of these three lie the stories lived and the stories told.

The Power of Story: Fairy Tales

Fairy tales are the quintessential expression of all three terms rolled up into story. They are pan-cultural stories that often yield moral imperatives. In many cultures, stories were transmitted over time transgenerationally by elders. Initially, before the advent of written language, they were shared and passed on verbally. This typically occurred in a given community with young ones, where their respected elders taught them proper and appropriate behavior, comportment, and righteous living.

Fairy tales often include warnings about what not to do, lest evil prevail. The characters and characterizations in them offer perhaps the clearest rendering of archetypes in all of literature, in all its many forms. Fairy tales convey to children that some aspect(s) of themselves, their sibling(s), and their parent(s) could well be found in its characters. They are generalizations based on extrapolation. Let's take a moment to examine a few tales that integrate evolution, revolution, and archetype into a "holy trifecta" or triumvirate of features from which we may all draw some significant learnings.

Peter Pan. We've already previewed this fairy tale's main character in our previous discussion about the puer and puella aeternus/a. While not a fairy tale in the traditional sense, Peter Pan is an archetypally evocative story, written on the cusp of the 20th century by Scottish novelist J.M. Barrie, about a free and spirited mischievous young boy who can fly, and never grows up. He spends his never-ending childhood having adventures on the mythical island of Neverland as the leader of the Lost Boys, interacting with fairies, pirates, mermaids, Native Americans, and occasionally ordinary children from the world outside Neverland. He is paired with his dearest and closest friend, Wendy, throughout the book.

In Barrie's book, we see not only the archetype of the *puer* at work (or, rather, at never-ending play, which Piaget noted was indeed a child's "work"). Other archetypes present themselves in this tale: the trickster/prankster, the fool, the wanderer, and the lost soul. These archetypes manifest themselves in Peter and Wendy in particular, and other minor characters who move in and out of the story as Peter journeys around his universe.

Peter himself derives in part from Pan, a minor deity of Greek mythology who plays panpipes to nymphs and is part human and part goat. The god Pan represents Nature or the natural state of human beings, in contrast to civilization and the stultifying effects of socialization on human behavior.

The Peter in Barrie's story is a free spirit, as well. He is too youthful to be bothered or burdened with the tiresome effects of formal education, or to have an adult appreciation of moral responsibility, accountability, and ethics. He is the embodied archetype of the child who couldn't and wouldn't ever grow up.

Cinderella. Cinderella is a fairy tale of international and cross-cultural depth and dimension. There is even an entire volume that tells this tale according to no less than 14 different cultural narratives. Thousands of variants are known throughout the world. The Brothers Grimm popularized the story, based on the original writing of Frenchman Charles Perrault in 1697, but it has since been cleaned up so that little of the original viciousness and violence remains. (This is true of most fairy tales: they have been cleaned up so much over time, they are seen by some as sterile and lacking true depth.)

The basic synopsis is that, after her father unexpectedly dies, young Ella finds herself at the mercy of her cruel stepmother and stepsisters, who reduce her to the lowest form of housemaid. In fact, her name derives from an English baby's name meaning "Little Cinder Girl." Despite her circumstances, Ella refuses to despair. An invitation to a palace ball arrives, and gives her hope that she might reunite with a dashing young male stranger she met in the woods. However, her stepmother, not surprisingly, prevents her from going. Help arrives in the form of a kindly beggar woman with a magic touch for ordinary things.

There is old-world historical precedent here. In the final years BCE, the Greek geographer Strabo recounted a story about a slave girl, Rhodopis, who married the King of Egypt. Since that time, nearly 2,100 years ago, the story has been embellished to reach near-mythical status around the world. The word and name Cinderella has come to mean one whose attributes were at first unrecognized, or one who unexpectedly achieves recognition or success after a period of oppression, obscurity, or neglect. In modern parlance, the name itself has come to mean "persecuted heroine."

The archetypal characters presented in this global fairy tale are the maiden, the witch, the princess, the queen, the prince, the elite snob, the *bourgeoisie*, the spoiled child, and the slave, among others. Other, non-human archetypes that come forth are magic, liberation, midnight, luck, fortune, good and ill will, hope, despair, oppression, and desperation. All have meaning and play key roles in this tale. It is eternal and timeless in its scope, in that virtually all people can relate to one or more elements within it based on their own life experience.

A Final Few Words

These synopses and analyses of just a few archetypal figures demonstrate that, as both literary and real-world partners on our life-journeys, these various life-forces are deeply embedded in our human nature and our human condition. How are you reacting or responding to this approach toward th*ese* critical aspects that permeate our lives? What might you have to add to this way of thinking?

Finally, let's take another look at a topic that has been raised and discussed earlier in this book: the focus on change. First, all organisms, from the most micro and molecular, sub-atomic units to those far greater – planets, galaxies, universes, multiverses – are subject to the laws of change: birth, growth, aging, deterioration, and death.

As all of these changes inevitably occur, so, too, does the way that the entity looks, feels, thinks, behaves, and reflects energy. Thus, change takes place not only in the realm of reality, but in the perspective of the changed entity. Change itself is inextricably interwoven in every moment. As we've noted, change is inevitable, and as humans we draw conclusions as to its relative goodness or evil based on its consequences and what we must undergo to arrive at the end-point of change and transition. We know that we imbue any and all forms of change with attitudes and temperaments that have everything to do with the change(s) that occur and their impact on us, our loved ones, and those we may never meet. As we learn over time to embrace change, our ability to absorb and grow from it lengthens and strengthens our lives in myriad ways.

PART FOUR

Eleven

~

Journeying with Archetypes

The meeting of two personalities is like the contact of two chemical substances: if there is any reaction, both are transformed.
~ C. G. Jung

A First Look at Integration

In this chapter, we'll finally pair the two words in the title of this book: *journeying* and *archetypes*. We'll bring both together, just as we bring into our lives the full capacity to put both into focus. As we journey through our days, we meet, befriend, fall in love with, lose, reject, abandon, and rendezvous with archetypes, their patterns (and ours), and complexes. Thus, we are always building and rebuilding our archetypal totems.

This chapter will focus on the more general – even universal – ways that these two partners meet and greet, connect, refine, and change one another. We'll identify how they trade off on experience, awareness, and understanding. Ultimately we'll concern ourselves with how, together and separately, they create depth, dimension, and meaning in our lives.

There are two basic forces at play in the generation of the journeys within our lives and the archetypes that we live out through them: nature and nurture. We'll explore these one at a time. For sure, they are sometimes difficult to distinguish; on the other hand, upon deeper reflection, we know that all of our journeys are, to a greater or lesser extent, hardwired through our human formulas of DNA and RNA, genetics, heritage, and lineage. We must also consider other forms of such "hardwiring" that are within us, down to our very bones.

At the same time, it's virtually impossible for humans to grow up, and grow older, in a vacuum. There are simple and complex patterns of socialization, acclimatization, social and other forms of learning, inter-connection, and interrelatedness with other fellow humans. More discussion will follow in Chapter Twelve. For now, we'll be looking at the more general factors, which may well impact one and all.

We fuse with, are confused by, refuse, re-use, and sometimes abuse these entities and this package we now know as archetypes. They are with us whether we know it or not, and they dip in and out of our consciousness awareness throughout our entire lives. These archetypes may appear and disappear at both the most confounding and yet the most predictable of times.

Other than their existence, there is no universal pattern or formula for the what, the how, and the when – and even the why of archetypes in our lives. Yet, it's even less clear that that! There are indeed times when we do see and foresee the arrival or the disappearance of an archetype. Rites of passage and other rituals, as well as times of major transition in our lives may call them forward and amplify them with greater clarity and force.

Triggers in Our Lives

As we've already noted, when we act, react, verbalize, or otherwise express ourselves, we always have a "come from" place that is rooted in feelings, values, and deeply held convictions. More often than not, we react and respond to incoming data and information based on our perception of an experience from our past. We know that a trigger comes from the momentary memory or re-visioning of a frozen or unresolved experience of some sort from our past. Often we don't see a trigger coming, so it just hits us, ready or not.

Our efforts to respond are generally far too impulsive to prove healthy or satisfying to us. We're often staggered by something that we've just said or done. We may not even be aware that we said or did something. What we've done and how we have reacted to something may come as a surprise to us – and to many around us who've witnessed our impulsive action or utterance. This is called being "in the grip" of a trigger or a shadow moment.

Many forms of psychotherapy or treatment are attempts to address or redress elements of our past that are confounding and complicating our present. As such, we risk confrontation and conflict with aspects of ourselves, and certainly with any practitioner who may serve to intervene.

Everything that happens in the present (our "journey of the moment") also harkens back directly and indirectly to moments in our past. When triggered, more often than not we are reacting in the moment to something (or some relationship) that has not yet been fully resolved from our past – whether we know this or not.

Many, but not all, of our early childhood memories and experiences have been repressed or suppressed. Many of us have generally lacked resources or access to resources in our past (such as therapy or therapeutic interventions, wise adult counsel, and other forms of support (or "scaffolding") that might have helped us to more successfully resolve problems, issues, or conflicts. Left unresolved, we are at their mercy at unguarded or unanticipated moments.

Individuation: The Path Forward

Although we're late in the journey of this book, it's necessary to re-introduce Jung's seminal concept of individuation at this time. It's where the two terms, "journey" and "archetype," become thoughtfully and thoroughly integrated.

Individuation, according to Jung, is a lifelong process of self-reflection and exploration involving our ongoing growth and development: in fact, our living journey. Along the way, we encounter all manner of challenges, struggles, obstacles, internal and external monsters and nightmares, trials and tribulations. These form one strand that animates our lives. In addition, we experience dreams, fantasies, aspirations, successes, and joys.

We mark our lives with cultural, familial, religious, personal, and professional rituals and rites of passage to account for many of these. These rituals occur for a wide variety of reasons, whether in memorium or in celebration. While humanly created, some consider these markers as being divinely inspired. Whatever their source, such experiences are often transformational to ourselves and those closest to us.

It could be quite interesting and perhaps enjoyable for you to generate your own list of rituals and rites of passage that you have personally experienced to illustrate this point. Taken together, they are the hallmarks that form an experience that is both unique to you and a collective human experience.

As an avid lifelong and passionate photographer, I have long been fascinated by pathways and portals in the form of bridges, tunnels, and trails, both as they exist in their natural state and as engineered and implemented by human beings, and have taken countless photographs of them. In their place, there is always a story, 10,000 stories or more, of those who have trolled and tread there.

My imagination runs wild with Emily Dickinson's concept of "I dwell in possibility." The pathways and portals that we enter, and the continued dawning of our conscious awareness, is what comprises individuation as a lifelong process. These transitional entrances and exits bring travel and story, myth and archetype, and all manner of duality to the fore.

Revisiting *Oz* for a Moment

Perhaps one of the best known films and most beloved characters in movies that we see undertaking a journey of tremendous magnitude – and encountering all forms of archetypes on her journey – is Dorothy in *The Wizard of Oz*. As a young teenager, she embarks on this journey by being torn out of her home in Kansas by a tornado – not of her choosing, of course.

The characters and beings she meets with are both "film real" and archetypes: witches, a tin man (with no heart), a scarecrow (with a fearful heart), a lion (with "full heart" and courage, or not?), talking trees, munchkins, and, of course the Great and Omnipotent Wizard of Oz (more on him in a moment). The beauty of these beings is that they all have positive sides (manifesting their personas or "outer selves") and shadows, their dark, hidden, repressed, and often negative sides.

But it is not only these external manifestations that Dorothy meets. Within herself, she must confront her inner demons, her own pain and hurt, and the stories (of suffering) that she tells herself: lack of confidence, fear, anxiety, stress, terror, and such. We can relate to her easily, as we've all confronted these in different ways, at different times in our lives. They are components of the shadow side of ourselves. We know them, but we generally don't want to know more about them, if we can possibly avoid doing so.

These internal confrontations form the first set of tasks we must undergo in our lifelong individuation process. Jung often referred to these experiences as dark nights of the soul. At these times, we are restless, we cannot relax, we are edgy, and we rehash and rehearse our negativity over and over – and over – again. We are triggered by and held in the grip of our negativity.

We must do battle with our own pain and suffering. This is all an inevitable and usually, an unenviable aspect of the Journey. However, it is from our own discernment and insight in this undertaking that much of our growth, awareness, understanding, sensitivity, and empathy evolve.

The Great Wizard of Oz represents two polar opposites of ourselves. First, his persona, the outer self, is projected to be one of wisdom, knowledge, and traditional power. This is what he sounds like as we are introduced to him. However, when Dorothy's little dog, Toto, wanders over to him and draws the curtain away from him, the Great Oz is exposed – the Emperor is naked – for all the world to see.

And, as is all too often the case, it is his shadow that we meet: a lonely, small, shriveled, unkempt little man full of self-doubt and self-recrimination. He's not alone here, although he is more exposed than many of us as private citizens are. All his contradictions, paradoxes, faults, blemishes, and all too human flaws come immediately into our field of view. We *heard* his grandeur, and yet we *see* his suffering. There is great pathos within and surrounding him; it looks to us as though he wants to make a quick exit and opt out of himself, and even the film itself!

Positives and Negatives

Recall that pain and suffering are not the same. Pain is real, and it occurs in all realms of our lives: physical, emotional, social, and existential, among others. Yet, on the other hand, suffering is optional. Suffering is the perception (and not necessarily the reality) of our experience and the stories we tell ourselves that enhance our own negativity. This is something we have the potential to change, through therapeutic interventions and personal growth.

The universe of archetypes allows us an entirely different dimension for exploring our inner and outer worlds. In a sense, by bringing them into our awareness, we are taking an important step out and away from the most immediate and urgent events and details in our lives, while still remaining connected to them.

Archetypes afford us a different – and a larger or meta – perspective on our experience. We grow into them as they incorporate themselves into us. It is, in some ways, a beautifully mutual and beneficial relationship. But it's also precarious. All the larger aspects of life have positives and negatives – life-affirming and life-ending qualities: fire, air, water, earth, clouds, the sun, to name a few. They can all be givers and takers of all forms of life.

	Positive Aspect(s)	*Negative Aspect(s)*
Air	Needed for breath/life	Hurricanes, tornadoes, pollution
Wood	Fire, fuel, building	Fire, rot, damage to life/building
Fire	Heat, warmth, light	Used to kill, burn, destruction
Water	Needed for life	Flood, poisoning, pollution
Earth	Soil/growth, building	Eruption/quakes, poisoning
Clouds	Bring rain, soften heat	Cause floods, tornadoes, change air
Sun	Bring warmth, light	Causes burning, excessive heat

Archetypes have some similar characteristics. We can get too close to an archetype, and try to become the archetype itself: "I'm Jesus" or "I'm God" (so-called "complexes"). If you've ever seen George C. Scott in the movie *The Hospital*, he has manifested this spot-on. His enactment of the "I'm God" archetypal complex is magnificent: he walks down the median of a crowded and fast New York City avenue imparting to one and all that he is God incarnate, raising his cane over traffic and passersby, railing to all that he is omnipotent, omniscient, and omnipresent. Other similar complexes can be seen in actions and/or statements like "I'm in charge" or all-powerful, or the world's best and greatest lover.

In these instances, when we morph ourselves into an archetype or complex, we get so fused to it or them that we get confused. That confusion makes us quite vulnerable in a world where authenticity and autonomy are supposedly embraced. And, on the other hand, we may get so scared by archetypes and their power and meaning that we can virtually disappear.

Two More Literary Examples

Another literary example where the two concepts come together with great clarity is *Siddhartha*, a short novel written by Hermann Hesse in 1922. This book deals with the spiritual journey of self-discovery of a young prince in India by the name of Siddhartha during the time of the emergence of the Gautama Buddha. In it, Siddhartha undergoes many transformations and iterations involving both his internal emotional landscape and the outer world of his persona and material belongings.

Each aspect of his journey is both whole unto itself, and yet incomplete as far as each is part of the larger journey of his entire life-span. In each aspect of the novel and his personal growth and development, it is as if he assumes not only certain archetypes and archetypal patterns and complexes; he seems to fuse with them. Not surprisingly, this fusion leads to confusion, and periods of physical stasis and temporary emotional or social paralysis.

There is tremendous joy – and challenge – as he travels along the many bends in his life-path. He is stretched beyond his present capacity each time he fuses with (and is indeed confused by) each archetype within his personal totem.

Over his longer life-journey, Siddhartha's changes and transitions hold great potential for inner awareness and wisdom as well as personal deception and lack of self-understanding. As is typical for a journey of this kind, he must grapple with and move through many contradictions and paradoxes in his experience in order to achieve a greater sense of self and other along the way.

Le Petit Prince (The Little Prince), written in 1943 by Antoine de Saint-Exupéry, is another tale focused on journey, archetype, and transformation. The protagonist, a blond-haired puer-type character, travels the universe (planets, asteroids, stars) in search of friendship, love, and intimate relationship. His adventures are really more of a quest for what he seeks, and what he perceives he lacks within himself. He seems to connect with the archetype of the innocent prince, but he is at once both quite naïve and quite wise (another archetypal contradiction and paradox).

With each of the characters whom he meets (all manner of sentient beings, including a fox, a rose, and many "people"), he finds new personal messages, growth, wisdom, and meaning. Once done, he is on his way once again. Our little prince is the consummate wanderer or adventurer. All of the archetypes with whom the little prince interacts are in fact aspects of himself that he cannot see within himself, so he must meet them externally.

One of the lead characters in a lesser-known Broadway (New York City) show, *Carnival*, has a variation of this same story. A tortured and physically disfigured veteran of World War II, he is the master puppeteer in a second-rate European carnival. The protoganist in this show, Lili, befriends each of the puppets and becomes part of the puppet show in spite of her dislike for the puppeteer himself. At the dramatic climax of the show, she has the revelation that the different personalities of the puppets that she has come to know and love are actually aspects of the puppeteer, dark side and all. Unlike the Little Prince, it is his dark persona that is apparent to the world; he conceals the funny, vulnerable, and kind sides of his personality, but they come out in his puppet creations.

Such is, in fact, the case with many of us: we access and learn about ourselves from our human and non-human relationships, especially when we cannot see (or know, or feel) from within ourselves. Outer, worldly manifestations often help to open us up, from the outside in. Often, an externalized journey brings us the people, relationships, experiences, and archetypes we need for greater understanding, awareness, and vitality.

So it has been for Dorothy, Siddhartha, the little prince, Lili, and dozens of other beings, both literary and human. We would do well to remember the aphorism, "not all who wander are lost." Journeying, questing, and wandering are in fact some of the best experiences wherein we can find, restore, or establish ourselves.

The chorus refrain in the popular hymn "Amazing Grace," written by an early American slave trader, John Newton, speaks (or sings!) to just this point. Newton himself had a major revelation while sailing a boatload of Africans away from their home toward enslavement in the United States. His boat, the Greyhound, had been in the grip of a huge North Atlantic storm for several days. Greatly imperiled, Newton reflected deeply on March 31, 1748, found God's "amazing grace," and decided to turn his ship around and return his captives to their free lives in Africa. This song is a testimony to his own lived experience. Here is one of the first verses:

> *Amazing Grace, how sweet the sound*
> *that saved a wretch like me. . .*
> *I once was lost, but now I'm found*
> *was blind, but now I see. . .*

We shouldn't delude ourselves into thinking that the only way to move, to recover or discover ourselves, is forward. This may seem counterintuitive, that we can grow in our self-awareness and consciousness by moving in any direction, not only forward. After all, that is what progress is all about, correct? Well, here's another thought: sometimes we must go back in time: we must journey backwards to find ourselves, or to retrieve a piece of ourselves. Let's look at a few examples to enrich this concept. No matter what, it's still a journey, or part of a journey!

Flashing Back to the Future... and Back Again

The Curious Case of Benjamin Button, a 2008 Hollywood film starring Brad Pitt, explores a man's aging in reverse. Born looking like an 80-something-year-old, Benjamin grows into his youth. This is his reality, although he was born with all the wisdom he would ordinarily have accumulated over a lifetime. It's an unusual premise, but a fascinating one.

In fact, Jung stated, in direct contradiction to the prevailing thinking at the time, we are not born as a *tabula rasa* (Latin for "blank slate"). Rather, with his conception of the collective unconscious hardwired within us at birth, we already have a trove of knowledge, relationships, and understanding that our individual lives play out in unique ways. This is the case with and the character of Benjamin Button.

In the 1986 Hollywood film, *Peggy Sue Got Married*, the protagonist, Peggy Sue, attends her 25th high school reunion after separating from her cheating husband, Charlie. She regrets the decisions she has made in her life up to that moment, such as getting pregnant by Charlie in high school. When she faints at the reunion, she awakens in 1960. Given the chance to relive her life, she changes many things. However, some of her choices and decisions are more complicated, as she begins to see young Charlie's charm and true feelings.

In this case, a woman whose present is not satisfying to her has an opportunity to live and re-live her life through a flashback, using what she knows and applying it to the past that brought her to an unhappy place. In some ways, our own cultural metaphors and aphorisms bring us to wish for this: "If only I knew then what I know now..."; "Hindsight is 20/20"; and others you might be able to add.

The evocative archetypes Peggy Sue lived with in the earlier incarnation of her younger self are still there. In fact, they've remained exactly the same over time. It is Peggy Sue in the present, immediate moment whose outlook, perspective, and life experiences have grown and changed. Thus, the archetypal imagery and characters maintain themselves. She is left to work through her past feelings, triggers, and restimulation based on her growth and her own personal human evolution and revolution.

Flashbacks, a popular and critical element in all of the performing arts, are akin to this growth process. The flashback is a device that is utilized to look back in time with 20/20 hindsight. It enables us – through actors and characters – to be able to move forward in understanding and meaning-making. Examples abound, and are almost too numerous to mention. Here are but a few:

Kurt Vonnegut's iconic novel *Slaughterhouse Five* is a prime example of time-twisting, using convoluted flashbacks through its main character, Billy Pilgrim, between 1944 and 1967, to Billy's childhood and back again. It's complex and tough to follow – yet, it's his perspective and remembrance of a critical segment of his life's journey. Jung's autobiography, *Memories, Dreams, Reflections*, described in an earlier chapter, was somewhat similar when he first wrote it, although it was not intended as such.

In the film *17 Again* (2009), a high school basketball star with a bright future throws it all away to marry his sweetheart and raise their child. Almost twenty years later, his marriage has failed, his children see him as a loser, and he's going nowhere in his career. He gets an opportunity to address and confront his earlier mistakes and change his life when he is miraculously transformed into a teenager for a second try. In attempting to "fix" his past, he ultimately jeopardizes his present and his future. Thus, the aspect of time is not only linear, it is backward, forward, and even stuck on hold. Second chances don't always add up, much as we hope and might think they would, could, or even should.

In Rod Serling's *The Twilight Zone,* a television series from the late-1950s through the mid-1960s, time is stretched in all its dimensions. Many individual episodes drill down into concepts of time, effectively creating somewhat of a time-warp: the past morphs into the future with no present time. There are futures with no past, there is a present where the future is already known, as well. It's all a stretch, both for our imagination and of reality as we know it. As do the humans featured in these episodes, we are forced to deal with these odd time warps as we go about daily life, including our quests and our journeys as we experience them.

A Matter of Time

It's easier to see life as a linear and forward journey. We are accustomized to this through our human processes of cultural, familial, and personal socialization. Our minds and hearts work hard to categorize and clarify everything as much as possible. There's a word that signifies our reasons for doing this: to simplify. But there's no word to indicate its opposite: there's no such term as "complexify" –

although I've personally made many efforts to use and insinuate this useful word into our language! Apparently, we'd rather see things moving in one direction – onward, and forward.

Living backwards, in reverse, experiencing life regression, is awkward and seems dysfunctional, or at least problematic. But must it be? We hold many axioms declaring the opposite: "If I'd only known then what I know now…"; "You'll see when you're my age…"; and "I should've known better." These statements all put the past in front of the present – a backwards regression of sorts.

Time itself has archetypal dimensions. A character referred to as "Father Time" may conjure up visual images of what "He" looks like, how he appears in this gender-designated role. (Who decided the gender, and why? What would it look and feel like to speak of *Mother Time* instead?) In addition, as we have seen earlier, the English language has commodified time, offering a host of words to precede it: *spending, wasting, killing, passing by, sharing, holding, losing, throwing away, sacrificing, running away from, in, out, beyond,* and so on. This speaks to the fact that time controls us, as much as we may want or wish to be in control of it. (Father) Time marches on. . .

As we know, a journal holds thoughts, memories, reflections, dreams or fantasies, and the aspirations of our lives and our journeys. Whether they are chronological or achronistic, there remains a sense that time is passing, as the writer writes and the reader reads.

The extent to which we are conscious of this is dependent on a host of cultural and personally-specific variables. One is how – and whether – our host culture values time. Another is whether our religion/faith/spirituality invokes time as a consideration. A third is how our archetypal patterns or complexes exercise (or exorcise) time in their roles, one's own mood, temperament, and personality, as well as the pressures and exigencies of a given moment.

In many major motion pictures, clocks spin around, going backward or forward rapidly to denote the passage of time, a method for demonstrating flashbacks or dreams of a main character. Two examples are Charlie Chaplin's film *Modern Times*; similarly, as was noted earlier, *The Curious Case of Benjamin Button*, starring Brad Pitt and Cate Blanchett, goes backward in time.

Multidimensionality

Archetypes have many dimensions, and even more when they collude, synthesize, or synergize with one another in an endless set of potential integration points:

- One's cultural and personal perceptions ("Universal to Unique")
- One's personal and cultural realities and context (the facts with which one lives)
- History, heritage, lineage, past, and background
- Lifestyle choices and preferences
- Personality, mood, temperament
- Identity/identities that we select or are forced upon us
- The element(s) of time and space (dimensionality)
- One's inner psyche, including spirituality/religion/faith/beliefs
- One's current and in-the-moment experiences and observations

Think of all this as "baggage" for our Long Journey (life itself), and our shorter (experiential, emotional, spiritual, work/career, family) journeys. We carry a great weight of invisible materials and supplies, experiences and observations, as well as cultural nuance, with us at all times. It's no wonder that most journeys have challenges, along with learning and growth, attached to them. Sometimes identifying and perhaps even overcoming the challenge is the journey itself.

A Preliminary Note on "Free Will" and Volition

Finally, let's take on the question of choice, free will, and volition. Do we choose our archetypes, or do they find us – or something else entirely? Another way of asking this, might be, "Are our archetypes predetermined for us, or by us?" The good news is, we will have some in-depth responses to this query. The bad news (for the moment) is that they will appear in the next chapter.

In asking the question to conclude this chapter entitled *Journeying With Archetypes*, we became more cognizant of the idea that they – in whatever formation or combination – are always with us, whether retrievable in our conscious awareness or not yet accessible to us. The threesome is always in contact and connection: life's journeys, the archetypes that go along on them, and the human experience of both.

TWELVE

~

Journeying with Your Archetypes

*There are as many archetypes as there are typical situations in life.
Endless repetition has engraved these experiences into our psychic
constitution, not in the forms of images filled with content, but at
first only as forms without content, representing merely the
possibility of a certain type of perception and action.*

~ C. G. Jung

A Few Key Queries

In a sense, now, our journey is coming full circle. Finally, here is
the opportunity to consider the journey with archetypes in a more
personalized way, taking time to focus on your archetypes, and
several questions and responses related to you and yours. You may
find yourself grappling – or having already grappled – with many
of these enquiries. I'll offer them to you here as a blueprint for this
twelfth chapter:

- In what ways are your archetypes yours to choose
  and select, and to what extent have they been predetermined?

- What is the process for receiving your archetypes?

- Can – and do – your archetypes change over the trajectory of your lifespan? If so, how and when and
  why? If not, why not?

- How do your archetypes influence you and your life choices and decisions? And/or, do you affect these archetypes? If so, how and in what way(s)?

- How are archetypes transmitted transgenerationally, over time and space?

- Is there anything more, beyond archetypes?

These are large questions, for sure. And (unusual though it is for a professor!), I will profess to not knowing or being able to share answers. In a world of archetypes, and a life full of journeys, it is not formulaic – there is no one-size-fits-all that offers direct, specific, clear, unambiguous answers that suit everyone. You will need to find them for yourself.

Understandably, you may find this frustrating. Yet, what may be more meaningful in the long term are the *responses* that will appear in these next pages. They are my attempt to be inclusive, and evoke the larger picture rather than to appear factual in a way that might not, and perhaps cannot, appeal to all readers. This is a more inter-active process, which I hope engages you in inner dialogue, or with others in your circle(s) who may be reading these pages along with

Chosen or Predetermined – or Something Else?

The life-journey and the journeys within it that we make and we take are not always of our own creation or choice. Certainly we select some, but, as we've seen, there are surprisingly few (if any) that are indeed universal in terms of direct application to all humans over space and time – as in, "one size fits all." Are you in agreement here, or have you found any universals other than birth, death, journeying, and change?

Questions such as how we are connected to a life partner (if we are), where, when, or whether we pursue higher education, or what we choose to think, say, and eat – all may or may not be personal and individual choices. Many cultures and families still hold one or some of these as givens. Personal options and opportunities are not allowed, and are indeed disavowed. This, in itself, is of critical importance to understand. We have only our own narratives and those of the people closest to us to look to for the "what and how" of the journeys we take, whether by free choice or the predetermination of others.

The Question of Free Will

What journeys are universal? An earlier discussion of this indicated birth and death. Once life exists – birth – then dying and death are guaranteed to occur, for all sentient beings. For the most part, as we've seen in a previous chapter, everything else is up for grabs. We've explored the controversial idea that there may well be no other universal journeys or experiences that touch all human beings over time and space and other manners of human or natural construct.

The issue of free will versus determinism is as old as the human species itself. It continues to be hotly debated across faiths, families, and governments, and through the arts. There is no way to give an encompassing and definitive answer to this particular issue.

Even if one could find a way to do so, it is also a question of personal conviction, belief, and values. And what empirical evidence is there that can be provided for one side or the other? Clearly, it is beyond our scope here to argue persuasively for one or the other viewpoint. It is the nature versus nurture challenge on a more abstract, theoretical – and personal – level.

If we shift the discussion to more specific meta- and micro- levels, we can engage in thoughtful reflection regarding the opportunity to personally and selectively choose from the multitude of archetypes, along with their complexes, patterns, and totems. Remember when you were first asked, "What do you want to be when you grow up?"

Let's pause there. You might think it is, but this is *not* a universal question asked by curious parents, relatives, teachers, or mentors as a child grows slowly (or, as some parents might sigh, "all too quick-ly") into maturity. Many cultures around the world actively inhibit or prohibit such a question and the free-will options involved in a child's response. Whether because of gender, socioeconomic status, geographical location, birthright, order in the family, parental values, and more, not every young person will be asked, nor will they be given a choice. Acting and thinking freely for oneself is not as yet a universal experience or birthright.

In such places, assignments as to vocation, avocation, education, income, and so forth are mandated and carefully monitored by family elders or the government or the clergy. The penalties for straying and invoking one's own will may be stringent indeed, including death, murder, honor-killings, and assassination.

In other parts of our world, free choice as to any and all of life's experiences is encouraged, supported, and provided plenty of scaf-folding. Some see this as a birthright; others see it as a blessing, gift, and rightful human values unfolding. The offering, or earning, of these options and opportunities may or may not come from a "proper" education, training, or family upbringing. But they may be present nonetheless if the culture, and the adults and elders vested with authority and power, promulgate this as an activated belief and behavioral system.

An example of both sides of this issue takes place in the story, movie, and Broadway musical entitled *Fiddler on the Roof.* It is based on the short stories of Sholem Aleichem in Russia between the years 1894 and 1914. The story focuses on Tevye, the dairyman, and three of his five daughters. The context is about Jewish life undergoing rapid transition in the Pale of Settlement of Imperial Russia at the cusp of the 20th century.

Given the rapidity of social change, each of Tevye's daughters presents him with a bold challenge. It is for him to accept or reject their novel ways. Each of them dares to choose a partner for themselves, each for slightly different reasons, under differing circumstances.

Based on these unique aspects, Tevye is either prepared to accept or reject each daughter (and their choice of life partner). In two cases, he assents, although grudgingly. In the other, he excommunicates his daughter from any further contact, as the match is too outrageous for him. He ponders each relationship differently, based largely on how far each of his girls strays from the accepted norms of the day, his village, and his strong religious faith.

Through this example, the question of free choice versus determinism and fate lands firmly on the side of each of the three daughters having options and opportunities, choices and decisions, to make of their own volition. Upon hearing Tevye's desperate pleas, orders, and commands, each one opts to go in their own direction and path, disregarding their father and tradition.

Holding the power to freely choose the course of one's life obviously affects one's vision and understanding of the extent to whether free choice even exists. However, there is no one alive who can control, contain, or produce dreams except the individual dreamer herself or himself. Therefore, the question regarding free will and free choice focused on archetypes is somewhat different.

It is true that the degree of free will in one's daily life will have an impact on one's dreams, but, beyond that, dreams and fantasies have other generators that are often beyond anyone's control. Unless a person is chained and tethered, or spied upon 24/7, they will inevitably have experiences and observations that, if not shared, no one else will know about. That said, archetypes evolve from many sources:

- Dreams, nightmares, fantasies, flights of imagination

- Strongly inbred cultural motifs

- How – and to what extent – one's hardwiring ("Nature") affects one's personality/temperament/mood

- One's daily observations and experiences

- Exposure to literature and the arts, formal or informal

- One's idiosyncratic interests and learning

- One's proximity to and interest in religion, spirituality, and faith

- One's access to and familiarity with nature and the natural world

Free will to experience, engage in, reflect on, and return to one, some, any, or all of the above is absolutely unique – even for identical siblings. With so many variables, our uniqueness – and the uniqueness of our personal worlds of archetypes – is virtually guaranteed. This is true with or without free will.

With or without free will and choice, you may or may not come to know all of your archetypes, patterns, complexes, or totem at a given moment in your life. Many of them remain submerged, repressed, and unconscious, emerging at times and in ways that are unexpected to us. It may also be one or more of our archetypes acting up, coming out without our conscious and conscientious awareness. Hence: surprise, shock, even denial and resistance. And yet – who of us would ever deny that we've done or said or even thought something that we've regretted afterwards? The unconscious, wherein archetypes reside, is a most powerful force in our lives.

So, returning to the central question of whether and to what extent our archetypes are predetermined or chosen by ourselves, my considered response would be: it depends. There are always forces at play that we cannot control.

Similarly, there are always elements in our lives that are far stronger than our own individual life force. We may rail and resist, and fight back against them – and many of us do. Naturally, there are consequences. In both the short term and the longer term, our actions and activities may be – or be seen as – positive or negative. Over time, the consequences may change. That's on one side of the response to this question.

On the other hand, all of us, once birthed, do exert some relative degree of autonomy and independence. This is true even if it may not be readily perceptible to others. Even our terminology enforces this: are you familiar with our internal autonomic nervous system? Thankfully, it generally operates successfully without anyone else's, and even our own, intervention.

Given this information, there is always some relative degree of selectivity as to what archetypes we may choose to activate and bring forward. In doing so, we can personally highlight and cultivate specific archetypes within ourselves and out onto and into the larger world.

What is the process for receiving your archetypes?

We've established where archetypes may come from. This gives us some strong clues as to how we receive them. However, simply because they're "out there" – perhaps waiting for us – does not mean that we simply select or inherit all of them. Like anything else, some "fit" or "match" us better than others, whether we are drawn to them or they are drawn to us.

We all ignore or resist certain things that come into our personal spheres, knowingly or not. Likewise, each of us has a degree of attraction to other elements in the inner or outer worlds. We may choose to befriend them, to tame or be tamed by them. Recall the fox and the rose in *Le Petit Prince*. What are the low-hanging fruits in your world wherein you've selected or entered into certain archetypes?

We inherit or inhabit our archetypes not only through everyday and typical behaviors. That's too easy and simple for such complex structures. Along the large Journey of Life, there are times when we are more open, vulnerable, and receptive to integrating or incorporating an archetype into our psyche and mentality.

Integrating Fear as an Archetype along the Journey

When fear overtakes us, we sometimes become closed or shut down, and shrink or regress into old, early patterns of thinking, feeling, and behaving. There is a magnificent passage in Yann Martel's 2001 book, *The Life of Pi,* that describes our visceral reactions and responses to fear:

> …a word about fear. It is life's only true opponent. Only fear can defeat life. It is a clever, treacherous adversary… It has no decency, respects no law or convention, shows no mercy. It goes for your weakest spot, which it finds with unerring ease. It begins in your mind, always. One moment you are feeling calm, self-possessed, happy. Then fear, disguised in the garb of mild-mannered doubt, slips into your mind like a spy. Doubt meets disbelief, and disbelief tries to push it out. But disbelief is a poorly armed foot soldier. Doubt does away with it with little trouble. You become anxious. Reason is fully equipped with the latest weapons technology. But, to your amazement, despite superior tactics and a number of undeniable victories, reason is laid low. You feel yourself weakening, wavering. Your anxiety becomes dread…

Particularly at times of big transition, when we are pressed into manifesting whatever resiliency and access to our support systems actually exists, our souls are more open to change. This is true, even as we may cling to the status quo (for example, an abused woman remaining in a hostile and abusive relationship or marriage).

Sometimes, it takes very big shifts in our "normal" lives to welcome someone or something that holds novelty. That novelty, which may challenge our norms and routines, may turn to fear. If and when it does, we may turn to others for comfort. We saw this in *The Wizard of Oz*, when Dorothy took her loving and comforting dog Toto, along with the Tin Man, the Lion, and the Scarecrow into her entourage as she made her way to the Land of Oz and its wizard.

The question of risk and adversity, as well as risk aversion, comes into play as well. How willing and ready are you at any given moment to take a risk? What does doing so depend on for you? In your response, you may notice that you are more or less open to risk, depending on a host of personal and contextual cues and clues, and patterns of prior behavior – and your ability to access a support system if and whenever necessary. This is an aspect of our personality that in itself is part of an archetypal complex. We may look to and hope for a cluster of archetypes that will converge to help move us into, through, or out of a potentially hazardous or scary relationship or situation. There are times for all of us when we either have or wish we had angels circling around us.

Whatever our responses to fear and risk look like, whatever images come forth for us when we stare them in the face, they affect our ability to work with and work through these emotions. Is it a monster, a dragon, a knife, a former lover, an act of nature, or a deity? In themselves, these are archetypes. We may accept or reject them, and they may or may not get us to behave in certain ways. Fear and risk often conjure up old experiences, frozen and repressed feelings, or repressed memories. When this happens, we are in their grip unless we possess the internal and external resources to notice and then transform them, thus transforming ourselves.

From Fear to Play

It may seem a huge leap – even a paradox – to jump from fear into play. I am not being casual or even suggesting causality here. We know that there are some mean-spirited individuals who prey and play on our fears. Sometimes, we'll come across these terms when we read about world news and the world of politics, where "scare tactics" seem to be in the playbook of one political party or another.

Yet, who of us has never "played" with other people's minds, or "played tricks" on others? In the natural journey of life, play is both an activity and an attitude. Playing with others may not be an intentional negative or manipulative action – although it could be. But, in a considered sense, while on our journeys, we have to "play" with variables in order to make sense of our options, our opportunities, our choices, and our priorities.

Thus, play is not merely an action or an attitude: it is an archetype in itself. Some of us work in order to play; for others, play is work. For Piaget, play is the work of childhood. Play can come looking for us, in the sense of playfulness, rule-bending or rule-breaking, or a spontaneous letting go of ourselves and our super-egos. Or, we can go looking for it, when we need a vacation, a break, or a time-out from the rigidities of life and work itself.

Getting to play is a release of stress and tension. It is the other end of a continuum wherein we may feel trapped by tension, conflict, and stress. As such, we can balance or rebalance ourselves by playing or feeling playful energy.

Years ago, I wrote an article focusing on an unrecognized epidemic, what I named "Play Deficit Disorder, (PDD)" in adults in the Western world. In it, I described how many adults have lost their way to play, cutting themselves off from spontaneity, the worlds of the unknown, being without final product and outcome, and unable to let go of the formalities, structures, and organizing forces that we cultivate and honor as the behavior of grown-ups.

As we cut ourselves off from these aspects of living and life, we also struggle to maintain such playful endeavors as creativity, innovation, fun, laughter, joy, and being fully in the moment. These are all aspects of play, and components of leading a full and fully human life. They have an archetypal dimension that should be respected and entered into with appreciation and hopefulness – and gratitude.

More on the Reception of Archetypes

With all of this in mind, as we enter and proceed on our journeys, it's important to know and note that archetypes come to us and through us. This transpires whether or not we're ready to receive them, and whether or not we choose them. Receiving an archetype is not akin to going shopping. We don't always have time or options to select from among various sizes, flavors, colors, or other characteristics. Nor are all these variations always available!

Sometimes, we just have to catch up to an archetype, not understanding at first why we might be feeling so reactive or proactive as we journey on. It's there all along, and it may come to us at an opportune moment or not, ready or not. It may slide into our soul and psyche without our awareness or consciousness.

Only later might we notice why we might be thinking, feeling, or behaving in a different manner than before. Sometimes, we don't catch it ourselves; a friend or family member who knows us well might be the person to bring the change or changes to our attention, directly or indirectly.

Most of us have heard common stories – some made into books, others into films – that demonstrate this. In one, a woman who gets a job outside the home for the first time develops greater self-confidence and feelings of personal and professional competence, thus becoming more worldly, decisive, and independent. These changes have a strong ripple effect on her children, her partner/husband, and possibly her friendship circle. In another situation, a "military wife" must spend long periods of time running her household alone, with her husband away in military service. She becomes gradually more comfortable with her newfound decision-making power and authority, but this change sets up a potential and real conflict when her military husband returns home, expecting things to be as they were when he departed.

On still other occasions, we may consciously want, even covet, some particular object or someone else's way of being or doing.

We may feel jealousy or desire or emptiness without that known desirable. Our emotions may well be based on our perceived scarcity of whatever it is. We may cultivate internally a yearning for immediate gratification or fulfillment that consumes us in the form of an obsession, compulsion, or ongoing temptation.

Thus, "reception" of an archetype – and our integration or incorporation of it within our psyche – may not be a matter of choice and selection, and may or may not be a conscious process. There are far too many variables. Life itself is simply too complex. Regardless of how an archetype comes to us, however, we must deal with some aspect of change that arises within us as a result. A range of emotions may ensue: confusion, relief, release, joy, anger, contentedness, and beyond. This repertoire will be based on how the archetype came to us, along with the extent of our psychic readiness to embrace the archetype.

For example, the young child who is always playful and making pranks will be more willing to receive the trickster archetype. This trickster may arrive in a dream, a story/fairy tale, even something within the natural world. Her openness to this particular archetype because of a pre-existent and predisposed personality or behavioral pattern opens her up to taking on the eternal and collective qualities of this archetype. The young man who has just been rejected by all of the colleges to which he applied may take on the role of the fool almost as a compensatory response to his newly-diminished self-esteem.

In our lives, there is an ambiguity, a give-and-take, and an openness/closedness with regard to receiving archetypes. We may experience concurrent ambivalence at any given moment. Every Life-Journey, and every journey within that life, is marked with all manner of archetypal receptiveness, as on a continuum. Like the ocean, there is a tidal ebb and flow that is both predictable and mysterious. This is part of the power of archetypes, as well as part of their fragility. And part of ours, as well.

Ultimately, all of our skills, knowledge, education, training, and experience are intended to prepare us for one thing: to adapt to and adopt change as a matter of fact throughout our lives. Wherever and however we start our journey at birth, we will not necessarily end in the same way at our moment of death. We cannot know: life is not fully scripted, beginning to end. So, change is a natural aspect of the human condition.

As we grow and develop, so, too, do our interests, preferences, concerns, questions, wants, and needs. Along the Big Path, much like Dorothy, we engage with numerous people, events, and other beings; some become our intimate partners, while others may be only momentary acquaintances.

Can your archetypes change over your lifespan?

The constant interplay and interaction on our journeys is also true of archetypes. While we may have an archetypal totem at any given point, it is not fixed and static. This archetypal totem may remain central to us in any combination. Yet, our psyche has a way of welcoming, denying, repressing, or releasing it or any of its elements.

To add to this complexity, we may revisit an archetype at different points in our life: it may be both not a constant and yet a frequent visitor. We all build more than one archetypal totem during our lives. Within these totems, some individual archetypes may be more constant across them than others.

Try to imagine your own unique archetypal totem at this time in your life, as you read this book. This may take a few minutes, so be patient with yourself! What comes to mind? Now, take a deep breath, clear (or write down) what has appeared, and think back to yourself as an elementary-school student. What images come forth on *that* totem? Can you imagine a third totem upon your graduation from high school?

Across these totems, you may begin to see consistencies and constants. It's worthwhile to pay attention and see what you might glean from this review of your archetypal totems over time. It tells us a great deal about ourselves in a way we likely have never considered.

Are you the same person you recall at an earlier part of your life? What's changed? What's remained the same? What are the possible reasons for changes and shifts in your life, your mind, soul, psyche, spirit, and body? Psychologists say we change many times during the course of our lives. What may catalyze our change, whether we consider it to be positive or negative, is our desire, our *motivation*, to change.

Some change is inevitable, developmentally. Our bodies grow and develop and age over time, and there is very little we can do to combat this, try as we might. In the end, we all die. Our minds and intellect grow, from very concrete to relatively more abstract. Our social world may become increasingly large and more complex, as does our understanding of work and working in the world.

Nevertheless, if we *seek* and *desire* and even *wish for* change, it is more likely to happen. The change may not be guaranteed or warranteed the way we'd like, or when and how we'd like:

> *You can't always get what you want...*
> *But, if you try some time, you'll get what you need...*
> ~ The Rolling Stones

In much the same way, as inner representations of our deeper selves, archetypes evolve into, through, and out of our lives. At the same time, *archetypes live on forever,* a duality that may be a challenge to grasp. They are a regular, ongoing feature and function of the human condition. How and when and in what ways they embed themselves into any individual is a matter of that person's unique narrative. Jung said that the archetypes, as a key component of the collective unconscious, have existed as long as have psyche and spirit and mind in the core of each human being.

Some archetypes have greater and more intensive "staying power" in our individual lives than others. This is a function of multiple considerations, all at work at the same time:

- the extent to which a particular culture encourages or inhibits a given archetype, whether it is taboo or socially acceptable

- one's unique role and birth order within a family, and the responsibilities vested in them due to this stature and status

- a person's "wiring": temperament, mood, personality, pacing

- to what extent or degree someone "buys into" issues like faith, religion, spirituality, and other existential concerns and questions

- one's personal willingness to undertake or avert risk and vulnerability, both internally and externally

- one's ability to accept, reject, or avoid conflict, change, and transition personally and the lives of those around them

There are probably several more elements that could be placed on this list. Can you add to it based on your own life experience and observations? With so many aspects, it is, I hope, apparent that we are not fixed or static as homo sapiens. Neither is the world-at-large, nor anything on it nor around it. Our personal archetypes change as our lives evolve and revolve.

Not every archetype is subject to change based on the elements listed above. Despite life's multitude of transitions, some archetypes are stubborn and stay with us, despite our conscious or even unconscious desire to eradicate them: *"I'm sick and tired of being/acting this way"*;

"I'll do whatever it takes to change..."; I *so wish I didn't feel/wasn't feeling this way..."* and so forth. Other archetypes we want or crave either don't come, or come and go too quickly, or we don't know how to be in and sustain a relationship with them.

We've already visited the question of whether we can control our archetypes. We have seen that this is not something we have power over, no matter how much we desire it. It is the same with changes in all other aspects of our lives. I would posit that *life itself is about learning how to adjust to change with grace and wisdom.*

The notion that life has an arc, or a trajectory (formed in a parabolic curve), suggests some incorrect visual assumptions. In mathematics or engineering, these lines curve inevitably upward and forward, as in up and over somewhere where they started. Would that life could be so simple.

It would be innocent, naïve, and arrogant to assume that all change is for the best, that all transitions are positive and reasonable and good for us. Faith-based individuals might wholeheartedly agree that all may be for the best, and that we, as mortal and imperfect beings, have but to strive to understand and catch up this concept: God or some other supreme (or higher) being has the answers, the wisdom, and the knowledge.

It is equally true that changes in our lives may also set us back, or cause some degree of regression, whether momentarily, temporarily, or more permanently. If we plotted a line to represent our lives it would go up and down, and back and forth, and straight and round and zigzag. It's messy, unsteady, not neat. At the same time, we are consciously and unconsciously generating our own individual evolution and revolution, as we learned in an earlier chapter.

In the same way, archetypes can and do change throughout each of our lives. Recall that archetypes are not limited to any singular way of being or doing in our lives. We're looking more at patterns of behavior, interaction, communication and expression, thought and vision, feeling and emotion, intellect and understanding. All occur over time.

None of us is steady, consistent, and static enough to maintain and sustain only one way of processing, initiating, responding, or reacting to all data. Some among us may wish it – or will it – to be so, while others covet the opportunity to develop an ever-evolving set of diverse responses to incoming information. Many of our "practices" are designed to help us to move flexibly and fluidly in one direction or the other.

We all have our stories and journeys around trying to create such practices in our lives. As I've mentioned, in my life I have meditated, chanted, prayed, done t'ai chi, attempted yoga, and cultivated plenty of other opportunities to help to build grace and gratitude within my life. And I'm still building – it's always in the present tense, never past. It's never "all done."

For the vast majority of us, to think any practice has made us perfect, or that we have "achieved" nirvana, or samsara, or transcended any aspect/s of human frailty or reality, would be a moment of sheer arrogance. Life has a way of humbling us when it's ready, whether we are or not!

We may start out as a child-trickster, grow into an adolescent jester, and then, over time, morph into the wise old man. As we've seen, change is perhaps the one constant and universal across all lives, all of life. Whatever we are at the start of our lives, it is certain that we will not end there, even if we experience a premature death. This is a function of nature as much as it is a function of nurture. As do archetypes, change occurs from within, and beyond.

At the same time, we've all heard – and perhaps used – the expression, "Some things (or people) never change." And, holding duality in mind again here, this is true, too. For example, the *puer* figure and archetype with whom we've visited, Peter Pan, never, ever grows up. That's precisely why he and she have the Latin word "*aeternus*" or "*aeterna*" (eternal) by their gendered names, *puer* and *puella*.

The extraordinary composer and musician, W.A. Mozart, is not only the physical embodiment of the *puer*, but also of the archetype of the musical genius, having composed his first full-scale opera by the age of six!

Animal archetypes rarely change over the course of time as well: the fox in *The Little Prince*, is, and always will be, his fox-self. How we regard him, as animal and as archetype, has everything to do with our own childhood and extended life experiences as well as our culture's image of and response to foxes. Do you know anyone, living or fictional, who inspires or manifests an archetype that has not changed with time?

As we've seen time and again, people and their archetypes do in fact evolve, especially as they resolve life's rites of passages, meet challenges from within and without, and undertake risks that they overcome. The innocent, questioning child may well become the wise old man or the crone, over the arc of their lives. The young-at-heart hero or heroine may in fact recede into an introverted loner over time. Einstein went from failing mathematics in high school to becoming a world-renowned genius with numbers and physics as he grew up and aged.

While we may cultivate the archetypes in our lives, and then grow into and harvest from them, they are visitors to our psychic fields. We either honor them or dishonor them. That choice may be ours to make and carry out. But what comes to us is somewhere between absolute random and total predictability. If we are able to hold this duality with some degree of grace and wisdom, we will have made significant progress in our lives and in the long curve of the human race.

How do archetypes influence you?

Now we get to turn the tables, so to speak, and look at the impact and influence we (may) have on our archetypes. We are forces of nature. We are also forces of nurture! As human beings and in our human doings, we are able to do both great credit and great damage to our environment as we live in our world, and with all beings within it. We've each seen the wide continuum of good and evil. We bring all the images contained therein into our daily life, work, interactions, and our dreams.

We have the potential to be instrumental forces for positive or negative, and our archetypes may be seen as projections of our hopes, fears, aspirations, challenges, and desires in the past, present, and future. To be clear, *the archetypes themselves do not change – they are what they are – but the way we see them and thus the extent and the way(s) through which they may influence us will change, based on our attitude, our perspective, and our life experience.* This is a clear reminder that we are, and always will be, in ongoing and dynamic relationship with these elements in our lives and our world.

As we've already seen, fairy tales are a phenomenal resource to consider with regard to this question. We often imagine archetypes in action when we read or hear a fairy tale. As morality tales with strong ethical implications and directions, there are clear polarities in the characters that populate these tales. They are generally all one thing or another: no middle ground here!

In the vast majority of fairy tales, humans are good or evil; kind or mean; nurturing or icy-cold; dirt poor or rich beyond measure; popular or socially isolated; handsome, beautiful, or gruesomely ugly, even disfigured. Although I've inserted the word "or" between each component on their singular continuums here, it's much more likely that we would see and experience *both*, as complementary opposites that together complete a whole picture.

And yet, through what we might now call the literary form of "magical realism" perfected by writers like Gabriel Garcia Marquez and Isabel Allende, we see frogs turning into princes, witches turning into queens, and so on. To further these characterological changes, new archetypes become attached to the new, transitioned being.

For ourselves, fundamental shifts in our personalities may shift the relationships we have with the former or current archetypes that sit with us. Let's revisit, for a moment, the *Myers-Briggs Type Indicator* (MBTI)® personality/preference inventory/questionnaire. This questionnaire is largely based on Jung's seminal 1920 book, *Psychological Types*. As you'll recall, Jung posited three "polarities," each defining a continuum:

> *Extraverted (E)* – *Introverted (I)*
> *Sensing (S)* – *Intuition (N)*
> *Thinking (T)* – *Feeling (F)*

The mother-daughter team who developed the MBTI added a fourth, "umbrella" continuum, *Judging (J)* – *Perceiving (P)*.

Without going into technical depth, what's important to this discussion is Jung's view that psychological types are not mutable during our lifetimes. He stated that they may shift over time in their relative strength, but they do not go from one "side" (letter) to the other, across each individual continuum. The next generation following him, the neo-Jungians, were more conflicted about this. Some indicated that, given major transitions in one's life, there is the potential to "cross over," say from E to I, or from N to S, and so on.

As an example from my own story, following a significant change in my life, around the time one might call "mid-life," I found myself in a changed and highly charged state. I was no longer able to relate easily, fluently, or fluidly to former ways of connecting with myself or with others. For a while, I was uncomfortable and vulnerable within myself, much as other beings are when they morph from one thing into something else: caterpillar to butterfly, a snake shedding its skin.

I found that I was dreaming – and therefore relating to – new archetypes, and my life was now being more informed by them. New now were the hermit, the adventurer, justice, and temperance.

Distancing themselves from the core of my evolving self were the dreamer, the jester/trickster, the hero, and the rescuer. It was a fascinating, intriguing time. Had I not known about the MBTI, archetypes, and the Tarot, I would have been clueless, and my transition might have been much more troubling and taken far longer.

My major life changes (eruptions, disruptions, obstacles) transformed some key aspects of myself, and my relations with others, including archetypes. My inner child became much more activated and needed more care and attention. This attention came first and foremost from my friends, colleagues, and family members. But support also came to me in the form of books, movies, dreams, and, lo and behold, the new archetypes that I found I was curious about and befriending.

In a way, this type of process of archetypal transition holds some similarities to psychologist Elizabeth Kubler-Ross' *Five Stages of Death and Dying*:

1. Denial
2. Anger
3. Bargaining
4. Depression
5. Acceptance

These may all be viewed as varied efforts to control change, and to maintain control through change. After all, isn't change the transition or transformation from something (bringing in; birth or re-birth) to something else (letting go; death) and vice versa?

An awareness of archetypes often helps to foster a greater awareness of self. And, it's reversible: knowing ourselves (through our emotional and social intelligences) helps us to gain greater consciousness and clarity about what may be catalyzing or decreasing our motivations and actions and thoughts.

The choices and decisions we make over our lifetime are tens-of-thousands-fold. And they range from micro (what to wear, what to eat) to meso (what car or home to buy, what school to go to) to macro (career, job, life partner, health).

Unless we are force-fed or scripted in every aspect of life, then we are making choices on one, some, or all of these levels on a frequent, often daily basis. Our selections are based on and steeped in our values, life preferences, faith or religion or spirituality, cultural mores and nuances, and so much more.

Archetypes can serve us in many roles: as motivators, cheerleaders, exemplars, challengers, visions, and aspirations. They come to us in dreams, nightmares, fantasies, observations of ourselves and others, in the media, in the arts, and through our daily life experiences.

How are archetypes transmitted over time and space?

Each of us inherits and inhabits our archetypes in unique ways. It is of equal truth and importance to know that they are transmitted across cultures and generations. Because we each hold our individual definitions, interpretations, and engagements with each archetype, the ways through which they are passed on in the human chain of generations is similarly unique.

In teaching, discussing, even analyzing such archetype-rich public forums as fairy tales, myths, legends, poems, and short stories, we may either consciously or unconsciously share that they emphasize certain elements that we may find either appealing or atrocious or in between.

For example, some elders amongst us may identify strongly with the archetype of the crone, the wise old man, the wicked witch, or the king or queen. In passing down stories and their archetypes, we are each vulnerable to seeing or not seeing aspects that may be either clear or subtle. Thus, what we share with our young ones is more likely to be our own personal interpretations than statements of clear and unbiased fact.

Cat Steven's elegiac folk song, "*Father and Son*" evokes the teenage angst and need to break away from the confines of home and parental control and compares it with the wise father counseling his adolescent son to calm down, "think a lot, think of everything you've got, for you will still be here tomorrow, but your dreams may not..." Even coming from the same culture and family, each sees "life" in such varied perspective, with such profoundly differing priorities. It is heartbreaking to hear the two voices sing to one another, knowing change is imminent and their relationship will be tested through upcoming transitions. Listeners of different ages will identify with one or the other voice in this song, and sometimes both.

Over time and through our sharing, we may come to believe that our personal interpretations are, in fact, fact. We come to believe in their absolute veracity. Upon closer questioning, these "facts" may or may not hold truth or absolute truth. If not fact, then these opinions and interpretations are based on what we know, what we've experienced, what we've been told by others, and what we're afraid of. Furthermore, they may be what we want others to know, experience, and explore. The power and grace of any particular archetype lie largely with the person or source referencing it.

As youngsters, many of us have had the experience of playing the game "telephone," in which the originator whispers a message to the person next to them, and this person then passes what they hear to another, and so on. Generally (and this has almost always been my observation in a group of more than four people), the original message and the message that lands with the last person is often quite – and surprisingly – different. So, too, are the way archetypes and the stories that convey them passed on over time, space, culture, and sub-grouping. One might even add that this is a natural response to interpreting and delivering data that we each receive and are triggered by in very different ways. This is, among other things, the beauty of diversity and complexity in action.

In all forms of human communication, there are two basic elements: expression and reception. If it's more than a monologue or one-way lecture or presentation, then we enter into a "feedback loop" where exchanges between two or more people go back and forth, more or less. In the best of all possible worlds, each entity listens carefully, well, and deeply, without interruption or distraction to the speaker.

Imagine what a different world we would be living in if this were the case every day, with each interaction! What might the game of "telephone" look like – or sound like – if the purest and deepest listening were in effect all the time? We practice communication hundreds of times daily from both sides, although the proportion spent listening and speaking is not always evenly divided.

However, precious little time is devoted to teaching young people how to listen! How – and when and by whom – were you taught to be a high-level pure-and-deep listener and a truly effective communicator? Many of us would be hard-pressed to give a clear, concise, and truthful response without feeling awkward or even uncertain about our answer.

Most of us have relatively fewer problems when communicating and receiving accepted facts. Theories and intangible concepts present a greater challenge. When it comes to passing on archetypes, and their meaning, power, and role(s) in our life, we are in a highly subjective area.

The human activities of interpretation, understanding, responding to questions, and analysis are generally based on individual and cultural messaging that confers many shadings and perspectives. It enriches and deepens the qualities and characteristics of any given archetype.

Certainly we may interpret facts in different ways – and we do. But we're on even softer ground when it comes to an objective and straightforward definition or content-based response regarding archetypes and any one individual archetype.

It's important to note than many archetypes must go through a sort of "cultural litmus test": a screening within a given culture as to what is acceptable, what is preferred, and what is taboo. In repressive and socially conservative societies and cultures worldwide, "out-there" archetypes like the fool, jester, and trickster – or those based on capitalist socioeconomic class distinctions such as king, queen, prince, and princess – may be frowned upon. Because of this, they may be repressed or obliterated from one's individual psyche, soul, and spirit. Thus, they remain monitored and held in check by the authorities and powers-that-be, such that they exist only in the collective unconscious and are rarely allowed to activate or manifest.

On the other side of this continuum, collectivist and communal cultures will do all they can to inculcate young people with stories and tales of archetypes and images of happy, whole, exemplary models that exalt all that is righteous and good within it. Some examples include the soldier, mentor, worker, parent, and citizen archetypes.

The Orson Welles film, and its lead character, *"Citizen Kane,"* exemplify this archetype. Not all depictions of this archetype are exemplary, although we see the motif over and over again in literature, film, and the theater. As we've seen with virtually all archetypes, they have both their persona (or public side) and their shadow (often their private and suppressed/repressed side). Certainly, R.L. Stevenson's *"Dr. Jekyll and Mr Hyde"* manifests the negative citizen or self, as do other personifications of evil and moral stagnation or degeneration. In your world, who have you come to know who represents or symbolizes both the positive and negative sides of this archetype?

There is an anthropological phenomenon known as the *"Hundredth Monkey Effect."* I first learned about this phenomenon in a Ken Kesey novel of the same name. In his book, he presented this effect as an inspirational parable by utilizing a reverse anthropomorphism. It was based on the pioneering work of Lyall Watson in the 1950s and his finding that, when sweet potatoes were dropped from above and found by Japanese macaques (a type of monkey), one taught another how to wash and clean, then eat, the potatoes.

In time, this learning and teaching took place in locations where no monkey had ever found, nor washed, cleaned, or eaten these potatoes before. Watson and his researchers then applied it to human society and the eventuating of positive change within human culture.

The gist of the *Hundredth Monkey Effect* is that once information about something reaches a critical number in real time and space, that information can literally "leap" across those two entities or locales to end up somewhere else entirely, and cannot be definitively traced back to its original source. It seems almost supernatural, almost magical. Yet, numerous instances have been documented in the psychological literature over the past 60-plus years since Kesey first brought it into the public imagination and eye.

These days, information and data leap over voids due to the internet and other forms of constantly changing technologies. Most everything can now be traced down to somewhere, something, and someone, if one cares to track hard enough. But, going back in time to the world's pre-technological era, grand concepts like love and hope and honesty evolved pan-culturally.

Jung would say this holds true of archetypes, in that they reside in the universal cesspool of the collective unconscious. Our culture, our personhood, and our dreams and experiences bear them out on a conscious level. With all of this comes the cross-cultural, multi-generational experience of our evolving archetypes, through space and time.

Is there anything more, beyond archetypes?

Many concepts larger than the mere word itself have been linked to archetypes: universes, multiverses, constellations, patterns, complexes, and such. While actual empirical evidence of archetypes resounds across cultures, literature, the arts, food, the world of work, and in our customs, artifacts, rituals, and rites of passage, the question emerges: Is there more? What else is "out there"? Might there be other ways to come to grips with our human dilemmas, contradictions, para-doxes, and suffering? This final question in this chapter is indeed a big one – an existential one – and, for the present moment, we can only speculate.

There's a wonderful short video I often shared with my undergrad-uate and graduate classes entitled *The Power of Ten* (1977), based on the pioneering work done by the American husband-and-wife team, Charles and Rae Eames, back in the 1950s. It looks to each larger and each smaller level one degree of 10 going out beyond the human being, all the way out to "what's out there" at 10 to the 27th power (speculation, not yet empirically proven), and then homes in on the human body at 10 to the negative 19th power (speculation, not *as* yet empirically proven).

Since at that time little was known about the great beyond (no one had yet landed on the moon) or the great within (sub-sub-sub atomic particles at that microcellular level hadn't been researched at that time), the film simply attempted to address *potential* and *possibility*. It enabled and permitted us *the power to dream*, and envision worlds that we knew little to nothing about.

Trying to imagine and hold concepts and realities beyond the col-lective unconscious and archetypes is a similar sort of challenge. We have the creativity, the imagination, and the curiosity to contemplate, even to research and study, what might be "out there" at present, beyond our reach, one power of ten larger than the archetypal field.

It may well be that we should set out on this particular journey simply by looking at synergy: the power to make something new and stron-ger by blending two seemingly disparate elements. We're starting out with an assumption: *the whole is greater than the sum of its parts*.

In our present exploration, the world or field of archetypes – within the collective unconscious – is greater than adding each of an un-limited number of archetypes together. This may seem paradoxical – what could be *more* than an unlimited number? Yet, even our own universe has aspects and components within it that we don't know.

This makes the universe even more vast than our vivid imaginations can hold. The whole of it is greater than each part of it.

Consider that we use but a fraction of our brains over the course of a lifetime. Brain researchers have long held that the percentage is in the single digits. Yet the capacity – the potential plus the possibility – is there to utilize this organ more fully than billions of people have ever done.

Therefore, the very idea that the brain may indeed have a limit or capacity leads us to think about the modern-day necessity to access and utilize our computers, our cell phones, our other tech toys, and so much more. But something becomes true and real because someone, somewhere, imagines it, breathes it, tests it, theorizes about it, and then brings it to some form of reality, however crude it may be at first.

Archetypes were not highly thought of nor respected within the larger psychological community when Jung first conceptualized them and shared his observations *of* and experiences *with* them. Most radical thoughts and thinkers are ahead of their time, and misunderstood or even maligned at first. Many "traditional" psychologists initially dismissed Jung and his ideas of terms like archetype, individuation, shadow, persona, and collective unconscious as feverish balderdash, and mystical, even hysterical claptrap.

One explanation of its instant disfavor is that the very notion of the archetype brought psychology – a "hard science" at that time – into the realms of religion, spirituality, and philosophy. At that time, all of these were domains that held great (and unprovable) controversies within them. Another rationale is that it made people uncomfortable, since it was thought and postulated that archetypes could not be measured or quantified. A third reason may be that it was simply a subjective, culturally-animated subject based on the wackiness of its generator, and nothing more.

In the realm of human intelligence, curiosity, and creativity, the pendulum around innovation swings two ways: toward change, and against it. This notion, known as the Hegelian Dialectic, was named for Friedrich Hegel (1770-1831), a German philosopher, important figure of German idealism, and a contemporary of Karl Marx. The Dialectic notes that there is generally a progression of anything novel through three stages:

Step 1: *Thesis* (something new, or something stated in a novel way)
    –to–
Step 2: *Antithesis (= anti-thesis)* (the push-back to maintain and uphold the status quo, in part based on fear of change)
    –to–
Step 3: *Synthesis* (some new synergy coming out of some degree of integration of the *thesis* and the *anti-thesis)*

While Hegel himself ascribed this particular terminology to the German philosopher Emmanuel Kant, it was Hegel's writings that popularized its concepts. They hold true in most domains, including politics, art, psychology, engineering, public policy, and peace building.

It certainly seems to have been the case with many of Jung's "far-out" musings, which have become more and more mainstreamed into the core of commonly understood psychological postulations.

Perhaps the most appropriate response to the query, "Is there anything more, beyond archetypes?" might be our mind-set regarding them. Our mind-set regarding, attitude toward, and response to this query are entirely individual, as trying to convince anyone of anything in these realms may well become both isolating and annoying. At the same time, we have the capability as humans to ask intelligent, curious, open-minded, open-ended questions, and to ponder various perspectives and paradigms.

Thus, the question here is not one of capability, but, rather one of our own motivation and determination. As we grow and develop, our ways of seeing and using all of our senses and intuition evolve from simplicity and concreteness toward complexity and abstraction.

Archetypes, and all that they have to offer us, reside in the field of complex and abstract – and yet they are also, interestingly, simple and concrete. They are in all of our childhood stories and fairy tales, dreams, nightmares, fantasies, musings, the stories we tell and those that we hear and see.

Archetypes are also part of the way we envision our futures, articulate our aspirations, and overcome our challenges throughout our lives. To return once again to those phenomenal lines in St. Exupéry's *The Little Prince,*

It is only with the heart
that one can see rightly;
what is essential
is invisible to the eye.

Thirteen

~

Full Circle, Full Cycle:
The Journey Home to Self

Musings on Coming Home

Like most journeys, most quests, and most lives, we are now making our return: the cycle is becoming complete. The homecoming is to come home to our selves. In doing so, we are hopefully replenished, reinvigorated, and renewed, with greater understanding and a wider perspective than when we first set out.

Whatever visual images we might use to reflect on journeying with our own archetypes, it is surely not a straight line out and back. This being the case, there is a looping characteristic involved in the start and to the finish: somewhere along the way, we have changed or been changed by some aspect of the journey.

There are times in our lives when we are unconscious, and therefore unaware, of change. Change occurs both perceptibly and impercep-tibly across all aspects of our lives – physically, mentally, socially/relationally, spiritually, and emotionally. Often it is not until we are challenged, or when we find ourselves in conflict, that we get to note and experience the changes within us. Then, we are better able to perceive the differences in our responses, attitudes, progression of actions and behaviors, our ability to ask differentiated questions, the engagement of others to problem-solve, even how we do our own problem-solving.

Sometimes we are the last to see our own changes, no matter what they are. As creatures of routine, human beings are insulated from making and then living out change unless there is a felt need, desire, or force that catalyzes us to do so. And there may be a lag time between the change and our recognition of what has occurred. That's the "ah-ha!" at work – the dawning awareness that we've done something novel, or responded in a new way, or been propelled into something unanticipated. It's consciousness after the fact: not always, but it does appear with some degree of frequency for most of us.

Our trickster or jester archetype may appear without any warning: it jumps out of us, and others may reckon with and recognize it before we catch it, or catch up to it – a playful joke, a prank, "jumping the gun" on something of that ilk. Maybe it's a wholesome act of impulsiveness, or something prompted or triggered by what we've experienced or observed. Or, suddenly we'll say or think something that is wise and sage beyond our years or experience: kids do this all the time, and we adults marvel at the "wise old man" who is only four years old! Consider when your archetypes have led you in an all-new direction – when was the most recent time this happened? What were the circumstances – and what is/was the learning for you?

What does this time-honored, time-worn expression "coming home" mean to you? What, precisely, is a "homecoming"? Is it a matter of returning to a physical place, or is it coming full circle with a set of emotions that starts off and ends up with either the same or a radically new mind-set? Or is it something else in addition, or entirely different? There are multiple ways to observe, perceive, and experience a homecoming.

A "Typical" Homecoming?

Let's take, for example, one of the USA's best-known, if not most appreciated, of traditions: the annual rite of passage known as College

Homecoming Weekend. Usually taking place in the fall, and most often with a home football game against another school, this big event may look entirely different depending on which role or constituent group one belongs to:

Active member of the football team: Gear up, get into your uniform, and be ready to play your best game of the year in front of a raucous home crowd that includes a great number of proud alumni in addition to the usual fans. It's all about the game.

Cheerleader: Be ready to exhibit and perform your acrobatics with a crowd-pleasing routine, but stay out of the way of the players, knowing that, except for time-outs and half-time, the event is really about sports. Be prepared to help rally the crowd from the sidelines.

Alumni: They're mostly only here to exhibit pride in their *alma mater*. They're "coming home" to relive old and cherished memories from years past. They're engaged not as participants, but strictly as observers.

The Homecoming "Queen" and "King": To the extent that these archetypes actually still exist in present-day human form, the homecoming event is about showing themselves off in a display of grandeur and hauteur. They have been chosen by some clandestine process, and are honored for their looks, popularity, notoriety, and/ or contributions to the homecoming institution. For the King and Queen, this is an event where the spotlight shines on them.

The Wizards behind the scenes: These are the administrators, co-ordinators, coaches, and staffers who pull the event together and attempt to make it as seamless and smooth as humanly possible. These wizards meet for many months before this annual rite of passage weekend and do their utmost to collaborate with one another and the hundreds of other stakeholders committed to pulling off the perfect collegiate weekend. If they are even seen at any part of the overall homecoming weekend and all its many events, they are certainly in the background, keeping their watchful eyes and listening ears tuned for anything that could disrupt their carefully planned weekend. They might represent archetypes such as the worker-bee, the elf, diligence, and heightened awareness.

Each cohort or constituent group will have quite different experiences, even though they are all gathered at the same event. It's still a home-coming, but each person's connection to it is based on their unique and subjective role within it.

In a similar vein, the journey home to self enables us to observe and experience our own inner and outer journeys from several concurrent places. Sometimes we'll see ourselves in a paradox, a state of living contradiction. Coming home may be joyous, and sad as well – we're back with what is and who is familiar (could be positive, could be negative). To do so, we've had to break our ties with wherever we were before coming home (this could also be negative, or could be positive).

Coming full circle will often involve myriad complex emotions, sometimes going beyond the binary or duality we've spoken of before. Remember, it's not a matter of one *or* the other, but rather, a question of accepting the reality of one *and* the other. We know, intellectually, that this is more easily said than done, as most humans have been trained to take in and work with one emotion at a time. Holding two or more contrasting emotions concurrently is quite challenging, and sometimes unfathomable.

Harkening back to my college years, in the latter years of the last century, I experienced mixed feelings when I returned home to my family for a weekend from my college campus. With my newfound independence and autonomy, I was proud, pleased, and happy to share (and, yes, even show off) my growth and elevated status as a newly-minted undergraduate to my parents and younger brothers.

On the other hand, I found to my chagrin that my parents and kid brothers treated me the same as always, and I now saw this sameness as disrespectful: an old, static way of viewing me. Homecoming was a bittersweet experience. I found that my behavior regressed over the course of these earliest homecoming weekends because I could not outgrow what I saw as their close-minded perspectives on me.

I thought and felt that I had outgrown my former self, but they could not seem to see or sense this. This was a big "ouch" for me, and I yearned to return to my new home on campus as soon as possible. I suspect I am not alone in this memory, among those recalling the experience several decades later or more recently.

Bringing Ourselves Home Again

We come home in our lives, again and again, bearing all sorts of new baggage and new gifts. We also have new stories: stories of quests, conquests, relational encounters with all manner of beings, frozen and repeated images, and perhaps new emotional states visited. Often, we return with new skills, or refined skills at a higher level from the daily practice of working with them while "on the road." Any of these may be the catalysts for deeper personal change in our lives – or not. Yet, no matter what, when we have returned from a journey there is the opportunity and potential for change both on superficial levels and more intimately – within our soul, psyche, personality, intellect, and spirit.

While a given journey may be over, we may not yet be aware of changes having happened, or those about to transpire. The mind works in mysterious ways. Much as we'd like to, we cannot always account for its undertakings in a timely or articulate manner. Our growth continues to build within us even after our return, and our awareness of our ongoing development and changed perspective may not occur at the precise moment or day of our homecoming.

A journey is always a learning experience, whether or not we wish it to be. It will likely both stretch and stress us in ways that are expected or completely unanticipated. What comes home with us is often a surprise or serendipity of some sort, anywhere along the positive-to-negative continuum.

There are aspects about ourselves that rarely remain untouched, even unscathed, over the course of a journey. Let's take, for example, the shadow. At the commencement of a first-time type of journey, our shadow often casts a large projection over and around us. While of course there may be excitement, curiosity, and energy, the shadow within us also casts a large pall of doubt, trepidation, fear, and even negativity at the start. It's human and natural to fear what we don't know – and cannot control – in what lies ahead. It's best for us to hold the notion that much of this is inconscious, or at least beyond the easy reach of our consciousness and conscientiousness.

Some psychologists label this "anticipatory anxiety." As we enter into an event, activity, relationship – anything novel – some of this anxiety melts away, in part because we are now *in* the experience itself, and doing it. If we're fully present for an experience, at least – and at last – some of our energy is diverted *into* it and we're not so focused or concerned *about* it.

Much of our shadow is unconscious darkness based on our fear and our terror – whether based on past experiences or anticipation of the future. Recall the *Life of Pi* quote in the previous chapter – our anxieties and fears can overtake us in the moment and serve to distance us from ourselves in the immediate present.

In making our Journey and journeys, if we are moving forward – heading toward home and a deeper self – then we are confronting our fears along the way. Over time, we hope, we are building greater self-confidence and competence. And, whether we know it or not, we are likely bringing these new-found gains home with us as well.

Even if we have perhaps retreated or regressed in or out of fear, we must recognize that we have also, in fact, attempted to deal with it. We have made an effort through this journey (whatever it was) to engage as much as possible. This is, at least, a moral victory, if not a practical one! Sadly, however, it may get lost or buried under the detritus of negative self-talk. Rest assured: something positive is within us, and we have changed and been changed from each journey.

Retracing Our Journey and the Path Homeward

The path or journey home is rarely smooth or straight. I'd like to think that all of our learning, our observations, and our lived experiences help to prepare us to adapt to always-changing circumstances and situations. Our journeys call on us to continuously modify our activities, our behaviors, our words, and our attitudes. This becomes vital and critical if we are to cope with whatever is presented to us as we engage in our ongoing journeying through life. It is from our mistakes, misdeeds, and mishaps – intentional and unintentional – that we have the potential to learn and grow the most.

What is "home" to each of us? What does it mean, what does it look and feel like? And, what makes it different than other settings and milieus in our worlds? I'd like to include words like "safe," "secure," and "at ease" as part of its definition, but unfortunately it is not universally appropriate to do so.

Around the globe, many of us are not safe, secure, and at ease with home and homecoming. "Home" might be some place, and some people, we may wish to avoid. There are many, many reasons for this. And it changes over the course of our lives, because our personal situations and circumstances change greatly as well.

Home may be a place of comfort, of routine, of loving and intimacy, but it may not. It may have been, or still be, a place of restriction, lack of safety, fear, intimidation, and what we fear or dislike.

Most of us know unmistakably when we're home, and when we feel at home. There are imprints and markers of all forms indicate that we have reached this place, whether it be an emotional or intellectual or physical homecoming. It may be a small return, or not, and a hard landing, or not. We've all experienced all manner of homecomings.

Simon and Garfunkel's song, "*Homeward Bound*" evokes some of what coming home means:

> *Homeward bound, I wish I was homeward bound,*
> *Home where my thought's escaping,*
> *Home where my music's playing,*
> *Home where my love lies waiting*
> *Silently for me. . .*

Surely, what awaits us at home differs across each human being, and each day, and each chapter of our lives, and every homeward-bound journey. It could not be any other way. No matter what, we cannot be sure what and who awaits us as we return to that place and those individuals we call home.

For some, there is a degree of consistency; for others, each is different in one or more ways. There is no way to categorize what a homecoming is, or what it looks or feels like, uniformly. There is a knowing, however. We know when we've reached home.

Yet, what is the common ground for declaring this experience and this place home? Good or bad, soft or hard, solo or shared, whatever it is – we have returned to a place and a setting that is familiar, that is known to us, and that holds memory for us. It is a physical and emotional storehouse for many of our experiences. It brings us back to earlier times in our lives, even if they are very recent.

To get there, we must "arrive." "Arrival" and "return," then, may be about the same place. But the attitude when thinking about it in these two different ways is radically different. Awareness of this difference is a key part of understanding the immensity, and the concurrent intensity, of any journey. The key difference between arriving and returning is one of attitude.

Arrivals evoke novelty, adventure, even mystery and the unknown. Arrivals are a beginning, a start to something. One feels and senses energy and readiness upon arriving somewhere. There is something about a return that feels slower, coming back to a place or a people that we've known and been connected to over time. A return is, in itself, a form of arrival. Returning indicates an end, or a termination of some activity or endeavor, and has a sense of completion to it.

The entrances and exits along each of our journeys – we can refer to them as portals – may themselves be considered archetypes. Doors, fences, gates, screens (on computers or otherwise), windows, elevators, escalators, bridges, tunnels, paths, and roads, among others, are all markers along each of our journeys. There may be rituals attached to any of these to signify the passage of time, space, growth, something new and added, or something taken away or lost.

These rites of passage heighten the meaning of these portals in our lives. This may add further gravitas to both the small journeys and the Larger Journey. We may need to run, crawl, drive, dive, jump, or stumble through these portals, and portal rituals and the attitudes that accompany them become integral aspects of our journeys.

We have an option and an opportunity to use the new tools, practices, skills, and knowledge that we've accumulated over the course of each journey to try to ensure our safety and sanity as we approach home through our homecoming. Sometimes our previous practices and routines are so deeply entrenched that we cannot discern at first how best to effectively integrate new ways of doing and being into the homecoming process.

We may feel ourselves to not be quite ready or worthy to adopt new practices. If we are able to utilize them, then we are catalyzing and enhancing our process of growth and development as we travel along, whether or not we experience travail. New learnings across all the dimensions in our lives are best established through the incorporation of daily practices. Knowing what we've learned long the way is challenging; integrating the learning into our daily lives is an even greater challenge: old habits and routines die hard, since we are creatures of habit. This is true for homecomings as well.

One Final Look Forward and Back

Let's take a deeper look at what some daily practices might look like. We know, in advance, that because we are unique beings, the complexion and make-up of each person's practices are unlike any others. There is no "one-size-fits-all." Homecoming practices in particular depend largely on cultural mores and nuances, the individual's constitution, and their relationships.

There are all forms of reunification with family members, friends, and loved ones. They may be formal and public or informal and highly intimate. Some involve physical contact of all forms, others may involve verbal or written acknowledgements, while there are also rituals of welcome and appreciation that a loved one has returned from a period of distinct separation.

Think for yourself: how have you returned from your journeys, whether traveling outwardly or inwardly? To whom, what, and where are you returning? What do these homecomings require for you in terms of emotional, social, or physical presence? For any of these, was your return and homecoming one of your choosing and design, or was it forced on you?

Some of us wish for and want – perhaps even need – social connection with others upon our arrival. We may hope and desire to be re-initiated into life back "home," whatever that may mean to us. Thus, the physical presence of others is important to some of us. Others, who may consider themselves to be introverts, may seek a quieter, more private way to insinuate themselves back into their home and surroundings. There is no right or wrong about any of this. Our unique needs and preferences give each of us the individuality that brings greater diversity into our world.

As we come home, there is both a settling and unsettling of contents. We might have physical possessions to unpack, emotional catharses of which we are both aware and unaware to reckon with, physical and emotional let-down and letting-down to experience, new intellectual growth to somehow integrate, and spiritual awareness to incorporate into our homes, home lives, and relationships. There may be either a draw toward or a fear around any of these activities, based on the qualities of our journey and the quality of our home – as well as our perceptions of both.

The archetypes that have accompanied us on our journey may prove to be allies in the processes of homecoming and resettling. They have been guides, supports, beacons, symbols, and provocateurs along our way. They have come to us at various significant moments throughout the journeys we have undertaken.

Archetypes may remind us to ask questions, to call out for help and guidance. Additionally, they may provide us with various "gifts" of time, energy, clarity, vision, hope, and even prayer when necessary or appropriate for each of us.

At the end point of our journey, when we reach "home," our archetypes, their patterns, and whatever archetypal totems have evolved over time remain with us. They have helped us grow our wisdom, patience, any of the forms of intelligence, empathy, and many other human qualities. We have a much bigger, longer, and stronger history to turn to when it comes to the final moments of ending a journey and beginning a new one: our homecoming.

Now, we come back to Joseph Campbell's epic question: *Where are you in your myth?* We are always the richer for whatever journey we may make, however it comes to and through us. Journeys are teachers; they are also trouble-makers, problem-askers and solvers, challengers, and partners in life. It is simply not possible to live a life without journeying. Journeying is intimately and integrally connected and attached to life.

Along the way, the archetypes we meet – for the short or long term – accompany us, whether or not we know them or want them. They attach us to the realities, perceptions, dreams, challenges, and triumphs of the collective history of all of humankind. And, our journeys become part of our human record and narrative. They are embedded in us, and become a core part of our myth.

Our journeying and our archetypes grant us the precious opportunity to make and find greater meaning in our daily lives. Beyond all of the busy-ness, the hundreds of daily transactions and activities in daily living, archetypes and journeys add depth, richness, color, and uniqueness to a life lived. Consider these to be your most deeply intimate partners. They are always within you and always beyond you.

Afterword

Time, now, to exhale, if you need and desire to do so. You've completed the journey of this book; it's now a part of your lived experience. You'll decide, sooner or later, if the ride and the time were worthwhile to you. Reading it may have left you with questions and/or thoughts that you don't know what to do with or where to go with. Please note that this "Afterword" was written and compiled and lives in this space specifically for those of you who are feeling somehow impacted (hopefully positively so!) by the journey you've just traveled, and are curious to know more, and, indeed, to consider venturing out – and within – for other related journeys.

My personal study of archetypes and other things Jungian has taken me from my college days to and through several decades as a full-time academic and into my new world as a trainer, consultant, mentor, and author. Likely I'll continue to read, research, facilitate classes, groups, and seminars focusing on this theme for the remainder of my days. As my understanding of and experience with archetypes continues to evolve, so, too, does my active engagement with them. This is my personal "journey of a lifetime". And, as you're aware, journeys al-ways lead us into places, situations, and circumstances that we could not anticipate. New doors open as old portals close, and we sort through our options before moving forward.

To this end, I wanted to have some time and a few more pages here to share some resources with readers regarding how you may continue to deepen your fascination and learning about archetypes, Jung, and your life and world. What follows below is intended to reference purposes only, and is certainly not a comprehensive rendering of everything that exists on these topics. You may wish to explore one or some or more; these are simply a few of the many entry-points into further and deeper discernment.

Journals

Parabola. Quarterly journal focusing on articles, poetry, art, storytelling. Focuses each volume on a specific aspect of lived human experience from an intercultural, interfaith, Jungian/archetypal perspective.

International Journal of Jungian Studies. The Jungian Society for Scholarly Studies publishes an academic, peer-reviewed, electronic journal.

Jung Journal: Culture and Psyche. An international quarterly journal published by the C.G. Jung Institute of San Francisco, offering feature articles, reviews, interviews, poetry, and art.

The International Association for Jungian Studies publishes several different volumes under various titles and brands, including *The Journal of Analytical Psychology, The Journal of Jungian Theory and Practice; Jung Journal: Culture and Psyche; Jung: The e-journal; Spring Journal and Spring Journal books;* and *Quadrant.*

Journal of Jungian Scholarly Studies, published by the Jungian Society for Scholarly Studies. The JSSS serves to organize interdisciplinary conferences through which members can present scholarly papers, organize roundtable discussions, and provide interactive workshops.

Selected Books by C. G. Jung

Man and His Symbols
Modern Man in Search of a Soul
The Red Book
Archetypes and the Collective Unconscious
Memories, Dreams, Reflections. (Autobiography/Memoir)
Psychological Types
Syncronicity
The Collected Works of C. G. Jung (20 volumes)

Books by Noted Jungian Writers

John Beebe: *Energies and Patterns in Psychological Type;
Integrity in Depth*
Joseph Campbell: *The Hero with a Thousand Faces; The Power of
Myth; The Hero's Journey; The Flight of the Wild Gander*
Edward Edinger: *Ego and Archetype; Anatomy of the Psyche; The
Creation of Consciousness; The Christian Archetype: A Jungian
Commentary on the Life of Christ; Melville's Moby-Dick; The
Eternal Drama: The Inner Meaning of Greek Mythology; Arche-
type of the Apocalypse*
Michael Fordham: *Children as Individuals; Explorations into the
Self; Jungian Psychotherapy;*
Sigmund Freud: *On the Interpretation of Dreams; Civilization and
Its Discontents; The Ego and the Id; Totem and Taboo; Beyond
the Pleasure Principle*
Barbara Hannah: *Jung: His Life and Work; Encounters with the
Soul; The Animus: The Spirit of Inner Truth in Women; The
Archetypal Symboloism in Animals; Striving Toward Whole-
ness; The Inner Journey: Lecture and Essays on Jungian Psy-
chology; Ego and Shadow*
Joseph Henderson: *Thresholds of Initiation; The Wisdom of the
Serpent; Transformation of the Psyche; Cultural Attitudes in
Psychological Perspective; Shadow and Self: Selected Papers in
Analytical Psychology; Testament to the Wilderness*
James Hillman: *The Soul's Code: In Search of Character and Calling;
The Force of Character and the Lasting Life; Suicide and the Soul;
Re-Visioning Psychology; The Dream and the Underworld*
Jolande Jacobi: *The Psychology of C. G. Jung; Complex/Archetype/
Symbol in the Psychology of C. G. Jung; Masks of the Soul; The
Way of Individuation*
Aniela Jaffe: *The Myth of Meaning in the World of C. G. Jung; From
the Life and Work of C. G. Jung; Death, Dreams, and Ghosts;
Jung's Last Years and Other Essays*

Robert Johnson: *Inner Work: Using Dreams and Active Imagination for Personal Growth; He: Understanding Masculine Psychology; She: Understanding Feminine Psyhology; We: The Psychology of Romantic Love; Balancing Heaven and Earth; Inner Gold: Understanding Psychological Projection; Ecstacy: Understanding the Psychology of Joy; The Fisher King and the Handless Maiden: Understanding the Wounded Feeling Function in Masculine and Feminine Psychology; Living Your Unlived Life: Coping with Unrealized Dreams and Fulfilling Your Purpose in the Second Half of Life; Owning Your Own Shadow: Understanding the Dark Side of the Psyche; Femininity Lost and Regained; Contentment: A Way to True Happiness*

Emma Jung: *The Grail Legend; Animus and Anima*

Marie Louise von Franz: *Alchemy: An Introduction to the Symbol ism and the Psychology; Archetypal Dimensions of the Psyche; Redemption Motifs in Fairy Tale.*

John Monbourquette: *How to Befriend Your Shadow.*

Robert Moore: *King, Warrior, Magician, Lover: Rediscovering the Archetypes of the Mature Masculine; The King Within: Accessing the King in the Male Psyche; Facing the Dragon: Confronting Personal and Spiritual Grandiosity; The Archetype of Initiation:- Sacred Space, Ritual Process, and Personal Transformation: Letters and Essays*

Caroline Myss: *Archetypes: Who Are You?*

Clarissa Pinkola Estes: *Women Who Run with the Wolves; Untie the Strong Woman: Blessed Mother's Immaculate Love for the Wild Soul; The Dangerous Old Woman; The Gift of Stiry: A Wise Tale about what is Enough; Warming the Stone Child; Seeing in the Dark: Myths and Stories to Rclaim the Buried, Knowing Woman; The Power of the Crone; The Late Bloomer: Myths and Stories of the Wise Woman Archetype; The Joyous Body: Myths and Stories of the Wise Woman Archetype; The Red Shoes: On Torment and the Recovery of Soul Life; How to be an Elder: Myths and Stories of the Wise Woman Archetype*

June Singer: *Boundaries of the Soul: The Practice of Jung's Psychology; Modern Woman in Search of Soul*

Murray Stein: *In Midlife; The Principle of Individuation: Toward the Development of Human Consciousness; Transformation: Emergence of The Self*

Anthony Stevens: *Jung; The Two-Million-Year-Old Self; Private Myths; Archetype: A Natural History of the Self; On Jung: Updated Edition*

Marie Louise von Franz: *Shadow and Evil in Fairy Tales; Psyche and Matter; The Feminine in Fairy Tales; The Interpretation of Fairy Tales; Individuation in Fairy Tales; Archetypal Dimensions of the Psyche; The Problem of the Puer Aeternus; Archetypal Patterns in Fairy Tales*

Marion Woodman: *Dancing in the Flames: The Dark Goddess in the Journey to Conscious Femininity; Transformation of Consciousness; Leaving My Father's House:A Journey to Conscious Femininity; The Pregnant Virgin: A Process of Psychological Transformation; The Ravaged Bridegroom: Masculinity in Women*

Toni Wolff: *Structural Forms of the Feminine Psyche*

Polly Young-Eisendrath: *Hags and Heroes: A Feminist Approach to Jungian Psychotherapy*

Professional Organizations

Archive for Research in Archetypal Symbolism (ARAS). ARAS.org

Assissi Institute: Archetypal Analyst Program. International Center for the Study of Archetypal Patterns. Mystic, CT. **assissiinstutute. com, assissi@together.net**

Carl Jung Resources for Home Study and Practice. **support@carl-jung.net**

Institute of Transpersonal and Archetypal Studies (ITAS). London and New York City. **info@itas-psychology.com**

Jung Page. **cgjungpage.org**

NY Center for Jungian Studies. Offers travel/study trips to Ireland, Prague, Israel, The Hudson River in NY State, and other places of note with a faculty of practicing Jungians, scholars, researchers, and authors focusing on various aspects of Jungian psychology. **nyjungcenter.org/**

Pacifica Institute, Santa Barbara, CA. Hosts, sponsors, and facilitates credit and non-credit courses, workshops, and seminars om the graduate and post-graduate level on Jungian-related content and themes. **pacifica.edu**

And, finally, please consider reaching out to me as another resource – with your questions, reactions, and responses to my book. I'll be sure to do my utmost to respond within a week or less, best as I am able! My responsive email address is: **danielcyalowitz@gmail.com**

Glossary of Important Terms

[N.B.: * indicates this is primarily a Jungian term or concept]

[N.B: *Terms in italics are of a language other than English, and are so identified.*]

A priori: (Latin) Reasoning or knowledge that proceeds from one's theoretical deduction (thinking) rather than through personal and practical lived observation and experience.

* **Archetype:** A primitive image inherited and passed down from the earliest human ancestors and present as an element within the collective unconscious. Also considered to be the basis for instinctual patterns of human behavior.

* **Archetypal Complex:** Positioned within the aspect of one's self known as the shadow, this is a relatively undeveloped and unintegrated grouping of powerful and unconscious impulses and preferences that are held together by a strong emotion or tendency toward a particular feeling.

* **Archetypal Totem:** A clustering of animals or other beings found in the natural world that may serve as one's personal sources of identity, strength, power, and connection that helps one to draw meaning and define purpose for the soul and the individual's existence in the world.

Bequest: The action of bequeathing or offering something either material or immaterial, tangible or intangible, based on a request or ask or prayer from a sentient being. It is given and offered freely and without intent for payback or donation.

Chronos: (Greek) Referring to the human invention of "clock time", *chronos* is a quantitative way of measuring time, breaking down what is eternal into carefully segmented objective units that have been named seconds, minutes, hours, days, weeks, months, years, decades, centuries, and milennia. Archetypally referred to as "Father Time".

* Collective Unconscious: The part of the unconscious that is derived from ancestral memory and experience and is common to all of humankind over time and space. It is a universal aspect unknown to ourselves that is holding place for the entirety of human experience and observation throughout time and space, shared and held by all people.

Emotional Intelligence: (Goleman, *et al.*) The capacity to be aware of, contain, and express one's emotions appropriately, and to handle interpersonal relationships genuinely and with empathy.

* Individuation: The human process of personal transformation whereby the personal and collective unconscious are brought into consciousness by means of dreams, active imagination, or free association to be assimilated into the entire personality. It is a completely natural process for the entire integration of the psyche over the course of one's human lifespan.

Journey: A process of entering into a physical, psychological, spiritual, social, or intellectual adventure without a script or a known outcome. It involves traveling from a known place and time and involves movement of some sort, with a point of departure and embarkation to some from of homecoming as completion. It may include emotional, physical, psychic, social, and spiritual elements.

Kairos: (Greek) Associated with *chronos*, this term is considered the qualitative aspect of time, focusing on what is considered to be the right or opportune moment for an event to take place because it is considered to be propitious. Ity involves the taking of an action, or the making of a statement, at the best possible time.

Multiple Intelligences (Gardner, *et al.*) As opposed to the quantitative and fixed measurement of a human being's intelligence using a rigid and formal testing procedure and set of protocols, multiple intelligence theory provides eight potential pathways for learning, including linguistic intelligence ("word smart"), logical-mathematical intelligence ("number/reasoning smart"), bodily-kinesthetic intelligence ("body smart"), spatial intelligence ("picture smart"), musical intelligence ("music smart"), interpersonal intelligence ("people smart"), intrapersonal intelligence ("self smart"), and natural intelligence ("nature smart").

Myers-Briggs Type Indicator (MBTI®) Based on Jung's book and theory of psychological types (1920), this is a personal preference/forced-choice questionnaire that demonstrates the strength of one's individual tendencies toward one side or the other of four scales or continua: Extravert-Introvert ("E/I"), Sensing-Intuition ("S/N"), Thinking-Feeling ("T/F"), and Judging-Perceiving ("J/P").

* Persona: In Jung's system of analytical or depth psychology, this term indicates the aspects of ourselves that face both outwardly and externally, toward the world of people, places, events, and objects. It is the side and qualities of an individual that she or he most wants to show and share with others, whether consciously or unconsciously.

* Personal Unconscious: Includes anything that is not presently conscious within the individual, but might be so. It contains, in essence, contents that at one time may have been conscious but have disappeared by having been forgotten, repressed, or suppressed.

Puer (or Puella) Aeterna: (Latin) Male (*puer*) and female (*puella*) terms for the eternal child (boy or girl), who is forever young and is unable to grow up to become a responsible and accountable adult. A person of any age who manifests the behaviors and thoughts of a child, but who may be wholly unaware or this being integral to their personality and activities; or if aware, is unable to change them.

Quest: A process of searching for something material or immaterial, whether tangible or intangible, wherein one may undergo certain personal risks and/or challenges along the way; an expedition to accomplish a prescribed task.

Restimulation: An emotional response or reaction to an individual, event, or object in the present that evokes a past memory, image, or person. Restimulations are often below the level of conscious awareness and cause us to rigidly respond to a situation in the present from within a recorded emotion of a past event. (Harvey Jackins, *Re-Evaluation Co-Counseling*).

* Shadow: The hidden and socially unacceptable aspects of one's personality, which, through conscious and unconscious repression and submersion, are usually relegated to the unconscious. It may exert unconscious control over an individual's thoughts and behaviors, and erupt in a range of violent ways. The shadow represents the darker traits, impulses, and emotions carried by all human beings. With appropriate and timely support and awareness, the shadow may be used positively to catalyze and channel one's creativity, energy, and passion in the world.

Social Intelligence: (Goleman, *et al*) The ability to successfully read, understand, and translate people's vision and non-verbal cues and clues concerning their responses to events and information and to respond in an appropriate and timely manner.

Tabula Rasa: (Latin) Literally, "blank slate." The concept that newborns arrive in the world without any data, information, or awareness of the world, and must be taught, socialized into, and/or given everything by their elders and the world around them in order to begin to learn and comprehend the workings of the world-at-large.

Transgenerational Transmission: A sociological term indicating that information, data, stories, knowledge, wisdom, and learning are passed on from one generation of people to the next through diverse forms of communication and/or technology.

Trigger: A human emotional reaction or response to an event, person, image, memory, or thought that causes immediate and unconscious negative behavior and/or communication. Triggers may often get in the way, or delay the building of effective trust, relationships, connection, and understanding between individuals and/or groups, and may escalate negative backlash toward the person who has been triggered.

COLOPHON

~

This volume was designed and composed during the foliage exuber-
ance of Fall 2018 using Minion Pro, a
typeface from Adobe Systems inspired
by late-Renaissance type, a period of
elegant, beautiful, and highly readable
type designs.